Often a simple change in what we
Ricci illustrate how a switch from '
leads to increased motivation, accep
realization that errors are simply roadmaps pointing to the direction
of learning as the "power of yet" is embraced. As teachers and parents,
isn't this the mindset we hope for our children?

Patrice M. Bain, Ed.S., *co-author:* Organizing Instruction
and Study to Improve Student Learning and Powerful
Teaching: Unleash the Science of Learning;
author: A Parent's Guide to Powerful Teaching

Meg Lee and Mary Cay Ricci do something quite rare—they speak
both the language of the child and the language of research, without
an accent in either. This is an accessible, intelligent and practical guide
to understanding what goes on under the hood of a young person's
mind and motivation, and it provides many hours of reflection to the
dedicated reader.

Tom Bennett, *founder, researchED*

Parenting is the hardest job on the planet. Likewise, the research around
mindset is sometimes complex and confounding. Authors Meg and
Mary Cay manage to shine a light and provide a brilliant clear path on
how to navigate both in this practical evidence-based book that every
parent should read.

Bradley Busch, *chartered psychologist and director of InnerDrive*

MINDSETS
for Parents

All parents want their children to be successful, but success is not just about giving your kids praise or setting them on the right direction. Research shows that success is often dependent on mindset. That's where the updated edition of *Mindsets for Parents* comes in!

Designed to provide a roadmap for developing a growth mindset home environment, this book's conversational style and real-world examples make the popular mindsets topic approachable and engaging. It includes tools for informally assessing the mindsets of both parent and child, easy-to-understand updated brain research, brand new examples and prompts for self-reflection, as well as suggested strategies and resources for use with children of any age. Also included in this updated edition are book club questions, designed to get parent groups thinking and collaborating in order to make the most of these strategies.

This book gives parents, guardians, coaches, caregivers, and anyone who works with children powerful knowledge and methods to help themselves and their children learn to embrace life's challenges with a growth mindset and an eye toward increasing their effort and success!

Mary Cay Ricci is an education consultant, speaker, and author of *The New York Times* best-selling education book, *Mindsets in the Classroom: Building a Growth Mindset Learning Community*; its companion, *Ready-to-Use Resources for Mindsets in the Classroom*; children's book, *Nothing You Can't Do! The Secret Power of Growth Mindsets*, and a book for education administrators, *Create a Growth Mindset School: An Administrator's Guide to Leading a Growth Mindset Community*. She is a former teacher and central office administrator. Mary Cay holds a Master of Science in Education from Johns Hopkins University.

Margaret "Meg" Lee is a public-school educator, holding many roles from English teacher to school administrator to director of organizational development. Meg's work in the field of learning science led to projects with the Center for Transformative Teaching & Learning, the Education Writers Association, and the International Society for Technology in Education. She has written for *EdSurge*, *Impact: The Journal of the Chartered College of Teaching*, and *researchED Magazine*, and speaks at gatherings of educators across the United States and in Europe.

MINDSETS
Strategies to Encourage
Growth Mindsets in Kids *for Parents*

Second Edition

*Mary Cay Ricci
and Margaret Lee*

Routledge
Taylor & Francis Group

NEW YORK AND LONDON

Designed cover image: © Getty Images

Second edition published 2024
by Routledge
605 Third Avenue, New York, NY 10158

and by Routledge
4 Park Square, Milton Park, Abingdon, Oxon, OX14 4RN

Routledge is an imprint of the Taylor & Francis Group, an informa business

© 2024 Mary Cay Ricci and Margaret Lee

First edition published by Prufrock Press Inc. 2016

Library of Congress Cataloging-in-Publication Data
Names: Ricci, Mary Cay, 1960– author. | Lee, Margaret, 1974– author.
Title: Mindsets for parents : strategies to encourage growth mindsets in
kids / Mary Cay Ricci and Margaret Lee.
Description: Second edition. | New York, NY : Routledge, 2024. |
Includes bibliographical references and index. |
Identifiers: LCCN 2023034268 (print) | LCCN 2023034269 (ebook) |
ISBN 9781032507828 (paperback) | ISBN 9781003405931 (ebook)
Subjects: LCSH: Learning, Psychology of. | Education–Parent participation. |
Achievement motivation. | Child psychology. | Parenting.
Classification: LCC LB1060 .R4947 2024 (print) |
LCC LB1060 (ebook) | DDC 370.15/23–dc23/eng/20230722
LC record available at https://lccn.loc.gov/2023034268
LC ebook record available at https://lccn.loc.gov/2023034269

ISBN: 978-1-032-50782-8 (pbk)
ISBN: 978-1-003-40593-1 (ebk)

DOI: 10.4324/9781003405931

Typeset in Adobe Caslon Pro
by Newgen Publishing UK

Access the Support Material: www.routledge.com/9781032507828

DEDICATION

For my husband, Enio Ricci, with love to my partner in parenting.

For my kids, Christopher, Patrick, and Isabella—Live your life with a growth mindset!

For my late parents, Joe and Mary Ellen Marchione, with gratitude.

—Mary Cay/Mom

For my parents, Katherine Lee and the late David Lee, with love, gratitude, and admiration.

—Meg

CONTENTS

CONTENTS

ACKNOWLEDGMENTS

Both authors wish to thank:

+ Theresa Alban, Jamie Aliveto, Cindy Alvarado, Michele Baisey, Troy Baisey, Carol Bates, Kristen Canning, Linda Civetti, Maureen Corio, Eric Haines, Keith Harris, Tracy Hilliard, Mike Markoe, Karine Myers, Emily Parker, Kristine Pearl, Cheryl Peters, Donna Quatman-Wilder, Eric Rhodes, Mary Jo Richmond, Barbara Rudakevych, Brett Stark, Angela Thomas, Jodi Vallaster, and Brian Vasquenza.
+ Kearney Blandamer, Jeff Colsh, Lesley Stroot, and Anthony Welch.
+ Monique, Patrice, Noelle, and Cain.

Meg Lee wishes to thank:

+ My family—the Donegans, the Guineys, the Lees, the Pences, and the Penns—for love, laughter, support, and encouragement, and the "MESS girls," without whom I *would* be a mess.
+ Mary Cay, who brought me along on this fantastic journey. There are not enough words to thank you.
+ My work family, for understanding how to apply growth mindset research well and demonstrating every day the power of an evidence-informed school district.
+ Paul Dunford, Susan Garrett, Tracey Lucas, and Marty Rochlin, who taught me to have a growth mindset before Carol Dweck even coined the term.

+ Jim Heal, for believing that there is more for me to contribute to the field of teaching and learning and for keeping me safe on the Million Dollar Highway.
+ Molly Magner, whose friendly introduction in a Boston ballroom led to countless amazing experiences, adventures, and opportunities in the learning science world.
+ Glenn Whitman, for sharing with me with the most amazing group of friends dedicated to teaching and learning. You know who you are, NeuroNerdSquad!

INTRODUCTION

"Do the best you can until you know better. Then when you know better, do better."

—Dr. Maya Angelou

Don't skip this introduction. We know that people do—in fact, we do sometimes! But this one sets the stage for your journey with us in this book.

We wrote this book because we love children. As lifelong educators, we want every child to grow, learn, and succeed. If you have this book in your hands, you most certainly do, too—whether you are a parent, a grandparent, a teacher, a coach, or a caregiver. We hope to be part of the journey to help children develop and thrive. But it is important to recognize that, as adults, we're on a developmental journey, too.

When we researched and wrote the first edition of *Mindsets for Parents* in 2015, we had no idea what the next several years would bring, both to us and to the world. Mary Cay wrote another book, this one for kids—*Nothing You Can't Do: The Secret Power of a Growth Mindset*—and travelled around the United States working with schools and parent groups to help them effectively understand mindsets. Meg found herself deep in the international world of learning science, engaging with a community of educators and researchers dedicated to applying the most promising new information about how people learn to the way we teach. And both of us (and, no doubt, you too) found ourselves in

DOI: 10.4324/9781003405931-1

the twilight zone of 2020 and 2021 that was the Covid-19 pandemic! If ever there was a need for perseverance, that was it!

Our own developmental journeys crystallized our belief in the power of a growth mindset, while also illuminating some ways that mindset can be misunderstood or poorly applied. The quote that began this introduction is from the late Dr. Maya Angelou, acclaimed poet, author, and civil rights activist. It resonates with us because we recognize that adaptation of ideas and strategies is part of being informed by research. New discoveries about how people learn and what techniques show the most promise continue to enlighten our thinking. When we were asked to write a second edition of this book, we jumped at the opportunity to share our learning with you and to address some conditions that have changed for all of us since 2015.

What you'll find in this book is a practical, easy-to-read guide for establishing a culture of growth mindset thinking in your home, classroom, or playing field. We'll give you snippets of the research, but we promise you don't need to be a scientist or academic to understand. We'll share with you what works most of the time, but we'll recognize that there are exceptions. We'll identify some of the ways growth mindset research has been ineffectively applied so that you can avoid those pitfalls. And we'll also say from the get-go that we're educators, not psychologists or mental health professionals. That's good news for you because we know how to frame information to help you learn, but we can't begin to address every unique challenge a child may have and we encourage you to find a specialist who can work with you and your child when you have such a need.

Finally, if you're looking for a quick-fix for your child's frustrations, know that our collective expertise would advise that mindset is not a quick-fix. You can't order a computer program on mindset and drill it into your teenager, you can't send your college student a list of books to read about people overcoming obstacles, and you can't just focus on praising your child for accomplishing easy tasks. (You technically *could* do all of these things, but they would be just scratching the surface of growth mindset thinking.) Instead, you can join us on a journey to create a climate that fosters hard work, determination, and perseverance. It is a multi-faceted approach that takes time and effort, but it will be worth it! Our kids are worth it!

So let's start learning!

CHAPTER 1

WHAT ARE MINDSETS AND HOW DO THEY AFFECT OUR CHILDREN?

"I want to make sure my children never stop learning."

—Gina, parent of three

Have you ever caught yourself thinking any of the following about your children?

+ "Poor thing, she isn't very good at math. She must have gotten that from me."
+ "He takes after me in his sports ability."
+ "Math and science are his strengths. He doesn't do well in literature."

The way we think about and react to our children depends on our mindset.

What are mindsets? Thanks to the research of Dr. Carol Dweck, Stanford University professor of psychology, society is going through a shift in thinking about learning and intelligence. Dweck (2006) described a belief system that asserts that intelligence can be developed and coined the term *growth mindset*. Parents with a growth mindset believe that their children can achieve at higher levels—with

DOI: 10.4324/9781003405931-2

effort, perseverance, and resiliency. Learners with a growth mindset believe that they can grow their intelligence with hard work and learn just about anything. It might take some struggle and some failure, but they understand that with effort and perseverance, they can grow and succeed. Growth mindset adults and children focus on the learning, growth, and improvement—not the grades or trophies, not on looking "smart" or talented. A growth mindset home environment encapsulates the philosophy that there is enough success for everyone. Both parents and children learn about the malleability of the brain and what can happen because of practice, perseverance, resiliency, and grit.

Conversely, Dweck coined the term *fixed mindset,* which is a belief system in which one believes that intelligence is something you are born with—it is genetic, it is innate—and although everyone can learn new things, your innate level of intelligence cannot be changed. A person with a fixed mindset might believe that he or she has predetermined "smarts" or talents in a particular area, but not in other areas. A child or adult with a fixed mindset might believe that he or she will never be good in a particular subject or talent, or will be afraid to try something that he or she thinks is too difficult, or at which he or she fears failure. For people who do not perceive themselves as "smart," it becomes a self-fulfilling prophecy.

It is important to avoid classifying people into "fixed mindset" or "growth mindset" categories. Rarely does anyone fit 100% into a category—we are certain degrees of each, depending on the situation. We know of a teacher who has a very growth mindset when it comes to her students and her teaching. She believes that they can increase their skills and abilities in a variety of different areas and her classroom is a space where the word "can't" is rarely spoken. This teacher expects each student to put forth significant effort and believes that all can achieve at a high level. She is a model growth mindset teacher; however, at home, she transitions into a fixed mindset thinker when it comes to her cooking skills. In fact, she is so sure that she cannot cook, she unplugged her oven and uses it to store her books!

Growth mindset is one of three learning mindsets defined by the Student Experience Research Network (n.d.). From 2015 to 2023, the Network led research and scholarship around three learning mindsets: growth mindset, mindset of belonging, and mindset of purpose and relevance. Combined, these three mindsets affect the ways children engage in learning in the context of school (preschool through college) and the broader world. Of these three, growth mindset can be cultivated in a variety of ways in your home and your child's day-to-day development.

Think for a minute about your own mindset. A mindset is a set of personal beliefs and is a way of thinking that influences your behavior and attitude toward yourself and others. A parent's mindset can influence how a child feels about himself or herself and how he or she views himself or herself. (In chapter 2, you will find the parent mindset reflection tool to help gauge your parenting mindset.) A child's mindset affects how he or she faces challenges. A child with a growth mindset is likely to persevere even in the face of barriers. A child with a fixed mindset may give up easily and decide to check out of the learning process because he or she believes that he or she does not possess the ability to understand this particular new learning.

A fixed or growth mindset can directly affect family dynamics as well. It is not surprising to note that parents have a substantial impact on how children view themselves. Parents will often view their children through specific lenses: "Joseph was born knowing his math facts;" "Patrick has always asked good questions," and "Catherine just knows how to interpret a piece of literature." These are all examples of a fixed mindset, even though the statements sound positive. These statements describe who these children "are," not what they have done or the effort that they have put forth. Think of some occasions when you have thought or heard yourself describe your child in a way that rationalizes perceived weaknesses: "She is just like me; math was not my thing either," or "I can understand why he does not do well in reading; I never liked to read" (Ricci, 2018).

SHIFTING MINDSETS

Breaking down the belief that intelligence is static can be a challenge, but with the proper groundwork and education, little by little a mindset can shift. Expecting a shift in mindset immediately is not realistic; after all, some adults have had a fixed mindset belief about academic success for most of their lives. No fault to them—fixed mindset thinking was likely embedded in many of us from a young age. Even after someone has had a self-proclaimed mindset shift, he or she will need to make a conscious effort to maintain that belief. A fixed mindset has an elasticity that continually wants to spring back. For example, a twice-exceptional child (a gifted student with learning disabilities) called to share a college schedule with his mother who also happened to be an educator. The parent had a mindset "shift" several years ago and had proudly shared all she did to encourage a growth mindset environment within their home. The schedule her son told her about involved 8 a.m. classes and a course roster that included macroeconomics, international business, accounting, analysis of media, and management. His mother noted that the fixed mindset mentality buried within her wanted to scream, "Are you crazy? You are setting yourself up for failure!" Instead, she responded, "It sounds like a challenging schedule, and I know that with continued effort, you will be able to manage it." Believing that all children can succeed—with effort, persistence, and motivation—is the heart of this belief.

BREAKTHROUGHS IN BRAIN RESEARCH

One of the reasons for this shift in thinking about intelligence is due to the available technology and research that examines the function and make-up of the brain. Recent brain research negates the notion that intelligence is "fixed" from birth. Formal and informal studies demonstrate that the brain can develop with the proper challenge and stimuli. Other current research in neuroscience emphasizes the concept of neuroplasticity. Neuroplasticity is the ability of the brain to change, adapt, and "rewire" itself throughout our entire life. Anyone who has ever witnessed someone recovering from a stroke has had a front row seat in watching neuroplasticity. In the case of a stroke, for most patients, the brain begins the rewiring process almost immediately so that patients learn to speak and become mobile again; however, it takes the hard work and effort put forth in physical, occupational, and speech therapy for stroke patients to regain much of what they've lost.

You might compare this "rewiring" of the brain after a stroke to learning to navigate a different route on a familiar map. Even though the destination may be the same and the landmarks might be familiar, the brain needs to learn new pathways to accomplish the tasks that used to be routine. Neuroplasticity works both ways; it creates new connections and eliminates connections that are not used very often (Ricci, 2018).

> Neuroplasticity is the ability of the brain to change, adapt, and "rewire" itself throughout our entire life.

Over the last 30 years, scientists and researchers have discovered much more about the way brains learn, remember, and change over time. This understanding cannot help but inform the way we approach how our kids learn and our own parenting. It directly affects adults' beliefs and expectations about children's potential and achievement. When parents and children (as well as their teachers) learn about the brain and all its potential, they witness the impact that it has on learning and mindsets can begin to shift.

You might be wondering a bit about research at this point. We certainly did! As educators, it is important for us to approach studies about growth mindset and learning with a few things in mind. We are taking a *research-informed* approach. This means that we are considering what the scientists have learned through their studies, but we aren't stopping there! It is critical that we also think about the context of the studies.

Most cognitive scientists are researching in conditions different than those in your kitchen, in your car, or on your child's sports field. Just as every child is unique and different, we recognize that there is no "secret sauce" to developing a growth mindset culture.

Imagine you find yourself chatting with other parents in your neighborhood and everyone is sharing ideas for getting kids to eat more vegetables. You'll listen to these ideas through a lens informed by your conditions, too—you don't have time to implement Aniyah's mom's idea of having the children grow their own veggies, your budget might not allow a weekly farm co-op membership right now, and sneaking vegetables into macaroni and cheese will never make it past the sharp perception of your child! But the idea of a rainbow of raw veggies with a side of homemade ranch dressing—that's likely to work at your house. We're taking a similar approach with research as we share it with you in this book.

So, we have asked ourselves, "Did the conditions of the study look like the conditions that parents face daily? Were enough children involved? Do parents have the ability to do something similar at home?" Just as noted educator Dylan Wiliam (2019) said, "Classrooms are just too complicated for research ever to tell teachers what to do," we believe parenting is equally complex.

INTELLIGENCE AND MEASURING INTELLIGENCE

Is it possible to increase your IQ? The University of Michigan partnered with the University of Bern to conduct a study that looked at the possibility of increasing IQ. This 2008 study (see Palmer, 2011) required participants to continually play a computerized memory game that involved remembering visual patterns. Each time a different pattern appeared, the participants heard a letter from the alphabet in their headphones. They were asked to respond when either the visual pattern on the screen or the letters they were hearing in their headphones were repeated. The time between the repeating of patterns and letters became longer as the game became more difficult. The researchers found that as the participants had practice and got better at the game, scores on IQ-style tests increased (Palmer, 2011).

This research and other studies like it contribute to the understanding of malleable intelligence, a key factor in growth mindset and a concept many parents and educators struggle to understand. In general, adults do not have a lot of background in cognitive science. After asking several groups of parents and educators "What do cognitive abilities tests/IQ tests measure?", without exception, there was hesitancy in responding to the question. After giving sufficient wait time, a few responses were shared: "a child's capability," "how smart kids are," and "their innate ability." What was more surprising than their responses was the observation that so many of these parents and teachers just could not answer the question. There are many times that parents and educators are in situations where data is shared about a child and that data often includes cognitive scores from gifted and talented screening processes, special education screening processes, and/or IQ tests. Who knew so many people really have no idea what these assessments actually measure?

IQ tests and cognitive ability assessments do not simply measure an innate, genetic intelligence. They also measure *developed* ability. If a child has had opportunities to develop the kind of reasoning that happens to be measured on these assessments, then he or she will score in the high range. However, if a child has never had an opportunity to develop these specific reasoning processes, the outcome of one of these assessments may not be reliable. David Lohman (2002), professor of educational psychology at the University of Iowa, stated that abilities are developed through experiences "in school and outside of school" (para. 3). When parents and educators review these "intelligence" scores without understanding the limitations, assumptions may be made about the child and beliefs may kick in that place limits on the child's potential.

THE ROLE OF POTENTIAL
AND HARD WORK

Potential. It is all about possibilities and promise. However, the word *potential* is often used in ways that don't always make a whole lot of sense. Think of the phrases, "He is not working to his full potential," or "We will help your child reach his full potential." How does potential become "full?" Is it something that can be checked off on a report card? Potential can never be "full;" it is never-ending, and our possibilities are infinite. As a child grows, learning and experiences become more sophisticated and challenging, growth continually occurs, and potential is never reached because it is impossible to reach. Perhaps many thought Michael Phelps reached his "full" potential after his tenth Olympic medal in 2008—a feat he went on to shatter at the 2012 Olympics when he won eight more medals. Believing that intelligence, talent, skills, and yes, even athletic ability can be developed encourages these endless possibilities (Ricci, 2018).

We are all born with potential. However, we might have innate strength or capacity in one or more specific areas. These strengths can manifest themselves in many ways. Strengths can be shown physically, creatively, socially, academically, athletically, musically, and artistically— the possibilities are endless. Every child has strengths, and some children are born with a greater degree of specific strengths or talents compared to their peer group. For those children with outstanding domain-specific strengths, their strengths and talents deserve to be further developed. However, it is also important to consider that other children have the potential to work side-by-side or even surpass those with intrinsic abilities.

Strengths can be shown physically, creatively, socially, academically, athletically, musically, and artistically—the possibilities are endless.

Think of a time that it took you a little longer to learn a new skill. It may have been something that required physical coordination, playing a musical instrument, learning a new language, using a new piece of technology, or learning a new cooking method. Then, once you learned this new skill, it became a strength for you. In fact, you surpassed others who have had this skill for years. As an adult, you had the drive, motivation, and persistence to decide that reaching this goal was important to you and you were willing to put in the time needed to learn the skill. No one took away the opportunity to let you learn, no one told you it was "too hard" for you, no one told you that this was "not the right group, team, or art class" for you. No one put up barriers to hinder your learning. Yet sometimes we do all of the above. Parents, as well as our school structures, eliminate opportunities, communicate low expectations, and prematurely remove children from challenging environments. Many reasons exist for hampering our children's potential in this way. One major obstacle is how we often judge both adults and children by the *speed* at which things are completed (Ricci, 2018).

Our society has become one that values pace. The faster, the better. If we don't get our tall, decaf, skim, extra hot, caramel latte in less than 2 minutes, then we are annoyed. If our Internet connection is not instant, then we grumble or click fast and frantically. (Did you ever accidently order something twice due to your frantic clicking?) If a driver in front of us is not going at a pace we agree with, then we use the horn or moan out loud. If an educator or parent describes a bright child, then we might hear him refer to the child as "quick" and to those whose work is not up to par as "slow." When speaking to a group of educators in Baltimore County, MD, Carol Dweck stated,

> We are the only country in the world that says rushing through math makes you good at it. Other countries know that it is about depth and quantity of time spent working with the skills and practices. We don't spend enough time on the foundation of creating great mathematicians.

We need to step back, take a breath, and realize that it is not about how fast our children learn, it is about the persistence and effort that they put forth.

GROWING HOME ENVIRONMENTS THAT EMBRACE A GROWTH MINDSET

Developing ways to establish a home environment that promotes the belief that intelligence is malleable is the major goal of this book. All parents must genuinely believe that all children can be successful. At the same time, children must also accept this belief system. It is all about beliefs and expectations. One way to contribute greatly to both children and adults embracing this belief system is by learning about the brain and all its possibilities (see chapter 4 for information on the brain). Educating ourselves and our kids about the brain has a significant impact on effort and motivation.

WHY MINDSETS MATTER AT HOME

Carol Dweck (2010) conducted a study of middle school math students in New York City. The students showed positive growth when they believed that intelligence is malleable and when they learned about their brains. Studies have shown that many students enter middle school with the belief that we are all born with a specific, set-in-stone intelligence level or a fixed mindset (Dweck, 2010). Similarly, in one suburban school in the Washington, DC area working on changing its students' mindsets, it was determined through student feedback and interviews that more than 60% of the children entering grade 6 believed that they were born with specific academic strengths and weaknesses and that they could not change. Based on this statistic, the question to ponder was: *At what point do children transition to this kind of mindset?* This prompted a new study in the same school district (Ricci, 2018). Mindset data was collected in kindergarten classes. In the fall, kindergarten students were surveyed to capture their beliefs about intelligence. In all the classrooms surveyed, 100% of the children—including those from high poverty and from middle-class backgrounds— demonstrated a growth mindset.

They came to school in kindergarten thinking that they could learn and be successful. They were enthusiastic, full of promise, and ready to absorb social and intellectual knowledge! With that optimistic data in hand, information was collected in first-grade classrooms; again, students were surveyed to capture their thinking about intelligence. In this case, only 10% of students in the first-grade class demonstrated a fixed mindset. For the most part, these first graders replicated the enthusiasm of the kindergarten students with the exception of a few students who felt that some students were born smarter than others and that we cannot really change how smart we are. Time to move on to second grade. In these classrooms, it was discovered that 18% of the students demonstrated a fixed mindset.

Are you beginning to see a pattern? With every increase in grade, more and more students believed that intelligence was a fixed trait. They agreed with the notion that "Some people are smart, some people are not." But perhaps the most surprising result was the large jump between second and third grade. Of the third-grade students surveyed, 42% had a fixed mindset! Table 1.1 displays these findings.

TABLE 1.1
CHANGES IN FIXED AND GROWTH MINDSETS ACROSS GRADE LEVELS

GRADE	FIXED MINDSET	GROWTH MINDSET
K	n/a	100%
1	10%	90%
2	18%	82%
3	42%	58%

Source: Ricci, 2018, p. 11. Reprinted with permission.

This data sends a message loud and clear: We need to start instilling a growth mindset into our children as early as possible so they can maintain a belief system that communicates that everyone can succeed. Our children walk into the school building on the first day of kindergarten ready to learn, believing in themselves with all the optimism 5-year-olds can muster. We need to capture and sustain that mindset as they make their way through life. Now, how can we accomplish this?

> We need to start instilling a growth mindset into our children as early as possible so they can maintain a belief system that communicates that everyone can succeed.

Our experiences in education, combined with our research about learning and mindsets over the last decade, have led us to believe that it is largely the environment that children develop within that makes the most impact on their beliefs about their own intelligence, ability, and potential for success. This isn't something that can be created by putting a poster on the wall or watching a movie with an inspiring character; rather, it is a collection of many small moments and messages—from parents, teachers, coaches, grandparents, and friends—that helps to cultivate the kind of resilience and perseverance that children need.

The following chapters will provide guidance and ideas for building a growth mindset home environment. We met with a variety of parent groups representing a range of socioeconomic, cultural, and education backgrounds. We listened to concerns and solicited their ideas for the kind of support and resources that they would like to have available to them in a parent mindset book. It was clear from meeting the parents that they felt what worked for one child in a family might not work for another. However, one thing we know for sure is that it is not possible to create a growth mindset home environment until parents first reflect on their own mindsets. Use the ideas and resources in the chapter that follows as a menu of sorts to help you to reflect and to support a growth mindset home environment.

REFERENCES

Dweck, C. (2006) *Mindset: The new psychology of success*. New York, NY: Random House.

Dweck, C. (2010). Mind-sets and equitable education. *Principal Leadership*, 10(5), 26–29.

Lohman, D. F. (2002, January 9). *Reasoning abilities*. https://faculty.education. uiowa.edu/docs/dlohman/reasoning_abilities.pdf

Palmer, B. (2011, October). *How can you increase your IQ? Stay in school (or just play some memory games)*. Slate. www.slate.com/articles/news_and_polit ics/explainer/2011/10/increasing_your_iq.html

Ricci, M. (2018). *Mindsets in the classroom: Building a growth mindset learning community* (updated ed.). Waco, TX: Prufrock Press.

Student Experience Research Network. (n.d.). *Compendium of Studies that Measure Learning Mindsets*. Retrieved April 10, 2023, from https://stude ntexperiencenetwork.org/csmlm/

Wiliam, D. (2019, May 30). Dylan Wiliam: Teaching not a research based profession. [Transcript of speech to Glasgow in Partnership with Tapestry's Pedagogy & Equity Programme] *TES Magazine*. Retrieved April 10, 2023, from www.tes.com/magazine/archive/dylan-wiliam-teaching-not-resea rch-based-profession

CHAPTER 2

WHAT IS THE ROLE OF PARENTS IN DEVELOPING A GROWTH MINDSET?

"Learning about mindsets has changed my parenting for the better! My only wish is that I had learned about mindsets when my children were little!"

—Joe, parent of two

The first step that should occur before beginning to build a growth mindset home environment is to reflect on your present parenting mindset. If your home is a two-parent home, it is important for both parents to reflect on their own mindsets. It is very possible that you have a mixed mindset home—one parent may lean toward growth mindset thinking and the other toward fixed mindset thinking. If both parents do not live in the same home, the ideal would be to communicate the importance of a growth mindset to your child's other parent. It is also possible that your background or culture might have an influence on your beliefs about intelligence, work ethic, and/or expectations. Approach this reflection with an open mind. While reading chapter 1, you might have recognized yourself in the descriptions and examples

DOI: 10.4324/9781003405931-3

of fixed or growth mindset. If you are not quite sure, take a look at the parent mindset reflection tool described in the next section. The parent mindset reflection tool will help provide guidance as to what mindset you are drawn to as a parent.

THE PARENT MINDSET REFLECTION TOOL

The intention of this tool is not to make you feel that your parenting style is under attack or to make you feel guilty. It simply suggests where your reactions might lie: growth, fixed, or somewhere in the middle at this point in time. This questionnaire does not consider your personal history with your child or children or their unique personalities and perspectives. If you have seen some of the situations described on the reflection tool over and over and over again, you might react in a terse, frustrated, or fixed manner. If you have never experienced the described situation with your child, you may gravitate toward a growth mindset response given what you have already learned so far—or you might predict the reaction that you would like to have.

During a quiet moment, reflect on the questions and statements in the tool (see Figure 2.1). Try not to think about what the "right" answer is—if none of the responses reflect how you would react, choose the one that is closest or just skip it. We purposely have not asked you to add up responses and find out if—"Ta-Da!"—you are fixed or growth. Remember in chapter 1 when we said we have some areas in our lives where we are prone to one mindset or the other? There are likely areas of parenting where you tend to have more of a growth mindset and other areas where you tend to have a fixed mindset. When you finish reflecting and responding to the situations on the parent mindset reflection tool, compare your responses to the information in Appendix A (p. 159) and reflect on where most of your answers lie: fixed, growth, or somewhere in the middle (neutral). Some thoughts that might be going through your head after reviewing your responses include: "I didn't realize that I actually lean toward growth mindset thinking," or "I thought I had a growth mindset, but my responses lean more toward fixed." The purpose of this exercise is to help you to reflect on your own mindset in relation to common parenting situations.

PARENT MINDSET REFLECTION TOOL

After Reading each situation below, choose the response that comes closest to your own typical response. (Don't try to pick a "right" answer- be true to yourself.)

1. Your child comes home with an A on his paper. You say:
   a. This is awesome! You are so smart!
   b. Good! You know I expect "A" work from you.
   c. Wow! Your studying really paid off.

2. Your child comes home with a less-than-desirable grade. You say:
   a. I told you that you should have spent more time working on this.
   b. I don't know why your teacher is such a tough grader. You need to talk to them about this.
   c. How did you go about doing this assignment? What might you do differently next time?

3. Your child scores the winning point on her team. You say:
   a. I am so proud of you! They won because of you!
   b. Wow! All of that practice really paid off!
   c. You sure did get lucky! Good for you!

FIGURE 2.1 PARENT MINDSET REFLECTION TOOL

PARENT MINDSET REFLECTION TOOL   (CONTINUED)

4. Your child gets nervous and does not do as well as you expected during a performance or event. You say:
    a. You were terrific!
    b. It wasn't your best performance. I could tell you were a little nervous.
    c. I can tell you are not happy with your performance. What do you think you could do to be ready for the next time so that you will feel more confident?

5. You notice that your child is spending a lot of time trying to figure something out (a game, puzzle, app, technology, etc.). You say:
    a. You are working really hard trying to figure that out. I am glad you haven't given up.
    b. I think you have worked on that long enough. Just give up.
    c. Here, let me do that for you.

6. Your child is taking a virtual class while you are working from home. When you check on them, you notice that they have skipped the responses that require a lengthy response. You say:
    a. Tell me about your strategy. Are you saving the ones that require additional effort for last?
    b. Do you want me to help you come up with answers for the hard ones?
    c. Hurry up and finish! I have a Zoom meeting in a few minutes.

7. Your typically high-achieving child is not performing well in a particular subject. In fact, you notice that things are getting worse. How do you react?
    a. You try to figure out how others are performing in this particular class. Perhaps it is the way the teacher is presenting new information?

FIGURE 2.1 CONTINUED

PARENT MINDSET REFLECTION TOOL   (CONTINUED)

    b. You let your child know what the consequences (technology grounding, limited social activities) will be if they don't show improvement quickly.

    c. You talk with your child to try to figure out what is getting in the way of their learning (confusion, distraction, pace, etc.) and what might help them succeed.

8. You notice that your child is struggling with a task. You:
    a. Distract them with a different task.
    b. Let them know that struggle is OK.
    c. Help them with the task.

9. You notice that your child avoids a challenging situation (such as a game, a sport or an academic class). When you ask why, he states that it is "stupid." Your reaction to this observation:
    a. Ask why he thinks it is stupid and listen for fixed mindset thinking.
    b. Tell him that he doesn't have to put himself in these situations. He should just do what he is comfortable with.
    c. Let him know that it is okay if he can't do it yet.

10. Your child gets angry when she makes a careless mistake. You:
    a. Tell her to settle down and not get mad.
    b. Share a story about when you failed or made a mistake and learned from it.
    c. Get angry as well. She knew better.

FIGURE 2.1 CONTINUED

FIXED MINDSET PARENT? GROWTH MINDSET PARENT? NOW WHAT?

Your response to the parent mindset reflection tool suggest the way your mindset leans when it comes to parenting—at this moment in time. Mindsets can change—with deliberate practice and effort. If you have discovered that you lean toward growth mindset thinking, focus on the items where your thinking leans toward fixed, or is in the middle. If you have discovered that you lean toward fixed mindset thinking when it comes to parenting, think about how you might shift responses and reactions to the following areas:

+ grades;
+ sports/recital performances;
+ when your child is frustrated and/or struggles; and
+ your child's failures and errors.

And the most important responses of all, reactions to:

+ your own failure and mistakes, and
+ decisions you make about why and how you give up on challenging tasks.

> Mindsets can change—with deliberate practice and effort.

You may also want to look at Figure 2.2, the growth mindset feedback continuum. This reflection instrument breaks down responses into three areas: praise, perseverance, and resiliency. Look at the statements on both sides of the arrow and place a mark on the line indicating where you are on the continuum. Look at the areas where you placed a mark closer to the fixed mindset statement (left side)—you will have to give more attention to how you respond in those areas.

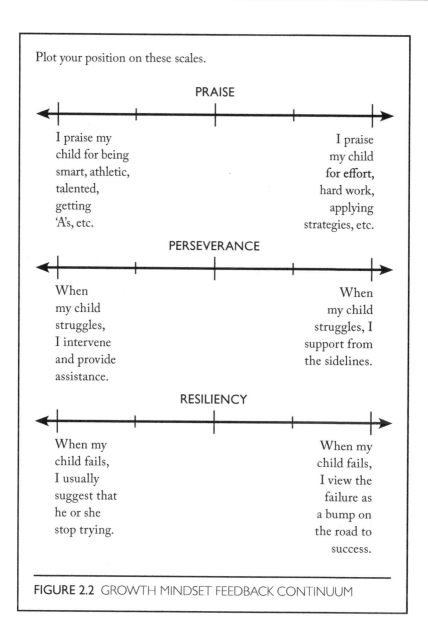

FIGURE 2.2 GROWTH MINDSET FEEDBACK CONTINUUM

THE PARENT'S MINDSET

Your own mindset has a tremendous impact on the mindset of your children, which is why we all must strive to practice growth mindset thinking ourselves. This sounds easier than it is, especially if we tend to lean toward fixed mindset thinking. When our kids see us face challenges, struggle, and persevere after setbacks, they begin thinking that routines such as these are just a part of life. They realize that just because we fail at something, we are not failures. We spoke to a father who shared that he was not comfortable letting his children see him fail. It was important to him to be the best role model and he wanted his kids to look up to him. It was not until learning more about the value of errors that he realized that he didn't have to always appear "perfect" in front of his kids. He recognized that if his children saw him make mistakes, reflect, and learn from them in a positive way that this message would have a lifelong, positive impact on them. The impact that your behavior has and the modeling you provide as parents cannot be underestimated.

MIXED MINDSET FAMILIES

It might be determined that one parent leans toward one mindset and the other leans toward the other. At one of our parent gatherings, a participant shared that having a spouse with the opposite mindset was like "sweeping up" behind the fixed mindset parent. The first step in reflecting on a growth mindset home environment is to realize that many times our parenting style is influenced by how *we* were raised. There are those who want to raise their kids the same way they were raised and those who make a conscious decision to do the complete opposite. According to clinical counselor Allison Bates, "We all come into relationships with our own belief systems from our upbringings, but it doesn't always mean it's the best way to raise your family" (Kadane, 2013, para. 4).

If you and your co-parent have different mindsets and decide to work together toward the goal of shifting toward a common growth-oriented mindset, like anything else, it is particularly important to keep those discussions behind closed doors and present a united front for your children. Begin with minor changes, like the way you praise and provide feedback to your kids. Chapter 3 will provide you with guidance regarding growth mindset feedback and praise. It is a first step toward a growth mindset home.

You may think that adjusting feedback and praise is an easy shift, but it could prove more challenging than you think, especially if saying, "You are so smart," "Brilliant!", "What a clever kid you are," and similar language are part of the lingo in your home. On a side note, grandparents are often the source of this kind of praise—after all, most grandparents think that their grandchildren are brilliant! Be sure to take the time to explain growth mindset praise and feedback to grandparents and babysitters. Let them know it is important to your family and is beneficial to kids.

For example, while one grandmother and her daughter, Maya, were out enjoying lunch together, a conversation began that proved to be a wonderful opportunity for Maya to share her parenting preferences with her mother.

Grandma: I was just telling my friend Mary how smart our little Sophia is—she was amazed at everything she is doing already!

Maya: Yes, Mom, Sophia is doing well, but let's keep the idea that she is "smart" behind the scenes. I don't want Sophia hearing that she is "smart."

Grandma: Well, why not? She is only 4 years old and she is reading already. In fact, when I posted that picture of her reading a book on Facebook, everyone was so impressed! I got a lot of "likes." *(Grandma beams.)*

Maya: I understand, Mom, but it is important to me that Sophia hears a positive message about the effort and hard work she puts forth. When we tell her she is smart, that communicates who she is, not what she does. I am concerned that if we keep telling her she is smart, when she is not successful at something she will become stressed and might not think that she is "smart" anymore.

Grandma: Well, you know I raised three kids and you all turned out all right. I always told you three that you were smart. *(She harumphs.)*

Maya: I am actually finding it a little challenging not to call her "smart" when she does something well. It takes practice, but it is important to me. So for now, let's focus on praising her perseverance and hard work. If you want to talk about how "smart" she is, we can keep that conversation between the two of us. *(She smiles.)*

This next dialogue is between a grandfather and his son, Dan. Both Grandpa and Dan were big track and field stars in high school and Grandpa has high hopes for his grandson, Emmet.

Grandpa: It's clear that the apple doesn't fall far from the tree. Have you seen how fast Emmet runs? He will be a third-generation track star!

Dan: Yes, Dad, he is fast, but he's not sure that he wants to pursue track.

Grandpa: What? But he has it in his genes! I was just telling him the other day how pleased I was that he inherited our running skills.

Dan: We've been working with a pretty powerful concept called mindsets, Dad. Emmet learned about it at school and it has helped him stay motivated and deal with any struggle he might face. Although it is important for him to know that you are proud of him, it would be great if we could just focus on how hard he is working during his soccer games right now rather than praising him for being a fast runner.

Grandpa: I'm just trying to make sure he knows that I think he's a natural track star! There is nothing wrong with that!

Dan: I know that you mean well, Dad. Emmet loves you and looks up to you. But as we've learned about mindsets, we've started to realize that Emmet sometimes tends to have a mindset that is fixed—he sometimes doesn't even want to try something if he thinks he won't be great at it. We want to help him to deal with the challenges he'll face by praising him for working hard, trying new things, and not giving up rather than telling him he's "a natural."

Grandpa: I really hadn't thought of that before. I think I remember you not wanting to try things you didn't feel confident about when you were his age, too. Remember your first experience with basketball? You wanted to quit after the first game when you didn't score any points. I'm still going to think of him as my little track star, because I'm the grandpa and I'm proud of him, but I understand why you don't want me to say that to Emmet.

Dan: Thanks, Dad.

Parents often struggle with the nature/nurture debate and can attribute a child's success or lack of success to genetics: "Oh, he is just like his grandfather, a born mechanic," or "I always struggled in math, I can empathize with her." As clinical psychologist and author Oliver James (2008) stated, "Simply holding the belief that genes largely or wholly determine you or your children can be toxic" (para. 1). Parents, teachers, coaches, scout leaders, and other adult role models should never blame genetics for perceived capabilities. If any adult in a child's life communicates low expectations either verbally or nonverbally, then achievement/success can suffer (Ricci, 2018).

Another important reason to educate ourselves about mindsets and malleable intelligence is to improve our own lives outside of our parenting role. According to Joel F. Wade (2012), author and life coach, adults with growth-oriented mindsets are also more likely to engage in more challenging tasks, to persevere, and to bounce back from adversity. Management teams with growth-oriented mindsets outperform those with trait-oriented mindsets. Also very interesting to note is that people with a growth-oriented mindset have a remarkably accurate assessment of their own performance and ability. Those with a fixed mindset have a remarkably inaccurate assessment of their own performance and ability.

> *Parents, teachers, coaches, scout leaders, and other adult role models should never blame genetics for perceived capabilities. If any adult in a child's life communicates low expectations either verbally or nonverbally, then achievement/success can suffer.*

Many large corporations have adopted growth mindset, including Microsoft. In June 2015, Microsoft CEO Satya Nadella sent out the following memo to Microsoft employees:

It starts with a belief that everyone can grow and develop; that potential is nurtured, not predetermined; and that anyone can change their mindset. Leadership is about bringing out the best in people, where everyone is bringing their A game and finding deep meaning in their work. We need to be always learning and insatiably curious. We need to be willing to lean in to uncertainty, take risks and move quickly when we make mistakes, recognizing failure happens along the way to mastery. And we need to be open to the ideas of others, where the success of others does not diminish our own.

(Rosoff, 2015, para. 5)

The *Harvard Business Review* (HBR), in reporting on how companies can profit from a "growth mindset" (based on a research project conducted by Carol Dweck), found the following:

Supervisors in growth-mindset companies expressed significantly more positive views about their employees than supervisors in fixed-mindset companies, rating them as more innovative, collaborative, and committed to learning and growing. They were more likely to say that their employees had management potential.

(HBR Staff, 2014, para. 5)

Implications from the study also suggest that growth mindset companies need to consider a potential employee's mindset when hiring. While hiring employees who demonstrate growth mindset thinking is important, what might be even more critical is the culture of the workplace when it comes to risk-taking, future opportunities, and improvement. Some organizations are shifting their practices to reflect a growth-oriented focus and the employee experience is changing as a result. According to author Jill Pearson, "Employees who work in organizations that they would identify as having a growth mindset are happier, more innovative, and more willing to take more risks" (Pearson, 2020).

As the above implies, the importance of our mindset goes beyond parenting. Mindsets influence almost every aspect of our life—even our relationships with our partners. Recognize fixed mindset thinking in yourself and talk yourself into a growth mindset place. This can also be done out loud so that your child can hear how you are changing your mindset. Other ideas include:

✦ If you catch yourself saying, "I can't figure out how to fill out this document," quickly rephrase it to add, "I think I need to check on the website or call the bank so I can ask some questions. Then I am sure I will be able to fill it out accurately."

✦ Be aware of your own fixed mindset statements such as "I am a terrible cook," "I was never good at math either," or "I wish I could play the piano like you do" (you can, with instruction, the right strategies, practice, and perseverance!)

✦ Be aware of blaming genetics for anything—both positive and negative. Be careful about comparing your children to their siblings or other kids.

✦ Model! We want our children to enjoy the process of learning anything—not just be successful. Model this concept at home.

For example, after a less than desirable outcome trying to bake something challenging, you might say, "I really learned a lot making those cookies," rather than, "Ugghh, what a waste of time! That was an epic fail. I will never try that recipe again."

✦ Redirect your child's fixed mindset statements. If you hear your child say, "I am no good in math," or "I just can't understand Shakespeare," point out the fixed mindset thinking and direct her to a growth mindset place. Remind her that she may not understand yet, but will by asking questions, finding new strategies, setting small goals, and working hard.

For more ideas, chapter 4 outlines the importance of communicating basic understanding of the brain and using that language with your child.

DISCUSSION QUESTIONS TO ASCERTAIN A CHILD'S MINDSET

Now that you have examined your own mindset, let's think about the mindset of your children. Young children naturally tend to have a growth mindset—remember the study mentioned in chapter 1? With every increase in grade, more and more students believed that intelligence is a fixed trait.

We need to start when our children are young and work toward sustaining their 5-year-old vision of their own possibilities and potential. How can we determine if our children lean toward growth or fixed mindset thinking? By observing, listening, and talking with them. Individually, with each child, pose some variation of the following questions. These questions can be used at all ages—you may just want to tweak a word or two depending on your child's age:

✦ Do you think that everyone can learn new things? Why?

✦ Do you think that some kids are born smarter than others? Why?

✦ Do you think that we can actually change how smart we are? Why?

> *We need to start when our children are young and work toward sustaining their 5-year-old vision of their own possibilities and potential.*

We expect that most children will agree with the first question, that all of us can learn. That is the warm-up question. When you ask if some people are born smarter than others, listen carefully to your child's response. Authentic responses of children include:

+ Some kids are lazy and just too tired for education.
+ Everyone starts on zero.
+ Everyone is born with the same smartness.
+ Kids are not born smart, they become smart.
+ Some kids are born smart in math and some are not.

If our children think that we are born with a certain level of "smarts," then that is fixed mindset thinking. If children agree that we can change and become smarter, then that is growth mindset thinking. Have a conversation with each of your children individually and make a mental note of where their mindset might be. As you begin to transition to a growth mindset home, bring questions like these up in conversation on occasion to gauge where your children are on the growth/fixed mindset continuum.

WHAT ABOUT GRADES?

If you are reading this during the school year, think about some recent conversations that you have had with your child. Did any of them center around grades on an assignment, test, or report card? Probably. So many of us overemphasize the importance of grades. We check online grades so often that we sometimes know how our child did on an assignment or assessment before they do! Grades suggest where your child is at *one* moment of time in *one* particular subject in *one* particular skill, concept, or content area. Grades do not predict a child's future or define their possibilities. A "bad" grade is an opportunity to reflect, regroup, and relearn. Grades are not consistent among teachers, do not always reflect student understanding, and most importantly, grades perpetuate fixed mindset thinking.

> Grades suggest where your child is at one moment of time in one particular subject in one particular skill, concept, or content area.

Traditional grades create a form of extrinsic motivation. Extrinsic rewards come from an outside place. Examples are things like money, stickers, and yes, even grades. Daniel Pink (2009), author of *Drive: The Surprising Truth About What Motivates Us,* explained that trying to motivate by promising rewards ("You will get an A!") has flaws. Often students will work to the point of obtaining the grade they want and no further. Intrinsic rewards refer to the personal satisfaction a person feels when something is accomplished, when no outside incentives are in place. The hard-working, persistent child who earns a B may feel more motivated than a child who receives an A without a whole lot of effort. Many of our children are so busy trying to make the honor roll or get the elusive A that they lose their love of learning. Jessica Lahey (2015), educator and author of *The Gift of Failure,* shares that from the first day of school we point our children toward an "altar of achievement" and train them to measure progress by means of points, grades, honor rolls, and awards (p. 20). We teach our kids that their intellect is more important than their character. We teach them to come home with 'A's, awards, and trophies. We expect college acceptance letters and scholarship offers. We teach them to fear failure, and that fear can destroy a love of learning (Lahey, 2015).

> Many of our children are so busy trying to make the honor roll or get the elusive A that they lose their love of learning.

By now we suspect that some of you are thinking things like:

+ "He needs to get 'A's so that he can get into the magnet program."
+ "But education is very important to our family, and we expect our children to be A students." (What we should expect is for our kids to work hard and apply appropriate strategies to learn—that may or may not result in an A.)
+ "She needs to get the best grades so that she can get a college scholarship; otherwise, she will not be able to go."

These are all valid reasons for wanting our children to be honor roll students and the fact of the matter is that currently in American education, grades can be a ticket to special programs and schools. However, there is a lot of chatter right now on social networks and in education journals that centers around the value of grades and, in fact, stories surface often about schools or districts that have eliminated grades. So, there is hope for the future! However, in most of our schools, grades are a reality for now. The most important thing to remember is to de-emphasize your children's grades and re-emphasize the process and effort they go through. The effort they put forth is important. More and more colleges and universities value interviews with students more than transcripts and Scholastic Aptitude Test (SAT) / American College Testing (ACT) scores. In fact, according to FairTest: The National Center for Fair and Open Testing, in 2023 more than 1800 4-year colleges and universities are "test optional" and don't require ACT or SAT scores to admit substantial numbers of bachelor-degree applicants. Test scores are not predictors of success. In some cases, the virtual interviews that have taken the place of tests at many of these colleges and universities include questions that gauge things like work ethic and perseverance—the things that contribute to success in college.

If your child happens to be in a school or district that has adopted a standards-based grading system, lucky you! Standards-based grading is often more growth-oriented and is more growth mindset friendly. Standards-based grading evaluates student progress based on mastery of specific learning targets (referred to as "standards"), instead of the traditional, A, B, C grades. You learn if your child understands a standard or is not quite there yet. This system gives parents and students more actionable information about what kids need to work toward. Other school-related issues are discussed further in chapter 6.

FLEXIBILITY AND OPTIMISM

Growth mindset homes are also ones where flexibility and optimism exist. People who practice growth mindset thinking tend to be more optimistic. What are some ways to make our homes places where flexibility and optimism exist?

+ Model flexibility. Communicate that change is an important part of living life. Model this by taking a flexible mentality when things don't go as planned. Don't let frustrating situations get the best of you. Instead, make your children aware of your ability to adapt due to a change in plans. Praise your children for their flexibility and adaptability when plans change or success is not instant.
+ Model optimism. Adopt a "glass half full" mentality in your home. A person with hope and an optimistic outlook believes there can be a positive side to most situations.
+ When things happen that are perceived as "bad," try to find the good in every situation. Have fun with it! For example, when a glass is accidentally broken, a light-hearted, response might be, "Now we have more room on our shelf!"

We should strive to be the adults that we want our children to grow up to be.

CAUTION! BEWARE OF THE FALSE GROWTH MINDSET

Sometimes, we think that we have a growth mindset, but our actions say otherwise. Carol Dweck (2016) and her colleagues have defined this as a "false growth mindset." We need to be aware of some of the things that we might do in the name of "growth mindset" but which are quite the opposite—they are fixed mindset actions. One of those things is telling our children that they are capable of anything: "You can do anything that you put your mind to, sweetheart." Yes, it is an important message, but when it is said, it is important to consider if your child has the experience and knowledge to make it happen. Dweck (2016) explained it like this: "While this may be true, simply asserting it does not make it so, particularly when students don't yet have the knowledge, skills, strategies, or resources to bring this about" (para. 8).

Dweck and her research collaborators have also found parents who value a growth mindset but will often react in a fixed mindset way. Dweck (2015) stated, "[parents] react to their children's mistakes as though they are problematic or harmful, rather than helpful. In these cases, their children develop more of a fixed mindset about their intelligence" (para. 12).

As you build a growth mindset home, be patient with yourself. Don't expect it to happen overnight. It is hard not to react to errors that our children make, especially when you think they should have done better. The trick is to react to the errors in ways that will cause your children to reflect, redirect, and rethink. For example, in a curious tone, ask your child, "What might you do differently next time?"

REFERENCES

Dweck, C. (2015). Carol Dweck revisits the growth mindset. *Education Week*, 35(5), 20–24.

Dweck, C. (2016, January 11). Recognizing and overcoming false growth mindset. *Edutopia*. Retrieved April 10, 2023 from www.edutopia.org/blog/ recognizing-overcoming-false-growth-mindset-carol-dweck.

FairTest: The National Center for Fair & Open Testing (2023). *Test Optional and Test Free Colleges*. Retrieved April 10, 2023 from https://fairtest.org/ test-optional-list/.

Harvard Business Review (2014, November). How companies can profit from a growth mindset. *Harvard Business Review*. Retrieved April 10, 2023 from https://hbr.org/2014/11/how-companies-can-profit-from-a-gro wth-mindset.

James, O. (2008, December 27). Genes don't determine your child's ability. *The Guardian*. Retrieved April 10, 2023 from www.theguardian.com/lifea ndstyle/2008/dec/27/family-medical-research.

Kadane, L. (2013, August 26). When parents disagree on parenting: What to do when you and your partner aren't on the same page about how to raise your kids. *Today's Parent*. Retrieved April 10, 2023 from www.todayspar ent.com/family/relationships/different-parenting-styles.

Lahey, J. (2015). *The gift of failure: How the best parents learn to let go so their children can succeed.* New York, NY: Harper.

Pearson, J. (2020). Engaging a belief in learning styles to encourage a growth mindset. *Performance Improvement, 59*(7), 19–24.

Pink, D. (2009). *Drive: The surprising truth about what motivates us.* New York, NY: Riverhead Books.

Ricci, M. (2018). *Mindsets in the classroom: Building a growth mindset learning community* (updated ed.). Waco, TX: Prufrock Press.

Rosoff, M. (2015). The buzzy new term at Microsoft is 'growth mindset'— Here's what it means. *Business Insider*. Retrieved April 10, 2023 from www. businessinsider.com/satya-nadella-instilling-growth-mindset-at-micros oft-2015-6/

Wade, J. F. (2012, July 6). Build a growth mindset. *The Daily Bell*. Retrieved April 10, 2023 from www.thedailybell.com/editorials/4055/Joel-F-Wade-Build-a-Growth-Mindset/

CHAPTER 3

HOW DO OUR PRAISE AND FEEDBACK IMPACT OUR CHILDREN'S MINDSETS?

"I love it when my mom says I'm a hard worker!"

—Sebastian, age 9

The word *praise* comes from the Latin word *pretiare*, which means to highly value or prize. This is appropriate because there is nothing that parents value more than their children. When we offer praise to our children, we may have a variety of reasons for doing it, but at the heart, we want our children to feel good and valued.

Feedback, on the other hand, is not designed to elicit the "warm fuzzies"; instead, it provides more specific information about how a task is performed, a statement that is made or an action that occurred, and is often used to acknowledge, reinforce, or improve a behavior. As adults, we regularly offer feedback to children in our efforts to teach them how to complete a task, refine a skill, approach something in a new way, or solve a problem.

Most of us don't spend a lot of time thinking about the language and purposes of praise and feedback—we just say what we think the child needs to hear at the moment. But if we take the time to reflect on praise and feedback through the lens of fixed and growth mindsets, we

DOI: 10.4324/9781003405931-4

find that there is a lot more to it. One element that we often overlook is to think about *what happens next in the mind of the child* after the praise or feedback is received. We need to anticipate how a child might react or what he or she may think immediately following the feedback or praise. The real power of praise and feedback lies in combining them effectively and choosing language that reinforces the growth mindset that we want to develop in children.

THE PRAISE PROBLEM

Carol Dweck's (2006) research uncovered that praising children for their ability pushed them directly into fixed mindset thinking and also diminished the pleasure that they experienced from participation in the experience. Let's consider the following scenario:

"You are such a natural hitter, Marco!" A proud mother clapped her son on the back as he walked away from the Little League field after a game in which he had three hits, two of them doubles. Marco's mother was excited and delighted about her son's great game and wanted him to know that she was proud and that she recognized his talent for baseball.

What did 9-year-old Marco hear? Marco heard a few things:
+ He's great at baseball.
+ He was born a good hitter.
+ His mom is proud and happy.

The real power of praise and feedback lies in combining them effectively and choosing language that reinforces the growth mindset that we want to develop in children.

What happens next? Marco likely won't see a need to practice hitting very often because he assumes he is a "natural" and doesn't need to spend time perfecting his skills. Marco enters the next game confident, but after he strikes out twice, he is confused and defeated. Why isn't he hitting the ball? He is supposed to be good at this! His mom even said so! She is going to be really disappointed to discover that he's not as good a hitter as she thought he was.

Did you notice that Marco's mom praised him for being "a natural?" That is what Dweck refers to as "person praise." When you praise the person for a trait like being intelligent or being naturally gifted at something, you convey the belief that the success is attributable to a genetic trait that the child has no control over. It is just like saying, "You are so tall." Being tall is not something that a child can control or change with effort, persistence, and hard work.

Instead, Marco's mom might have used what Dweck called "process praise." Process praise is directed at what the child *did* rather than who the child *is*. In Marco's case, his mom might have said, "Great hits, Marco! I can tell that your practice has paid off!" This message also conveys her pride in his accomplishment, but rather than tying the "why" to innate ability, Marco's mom has tied the "why" to his efforts in practice. This is likely to change Marco's next thoughts and next steps. He heard his mother attribute his great game to his hard work. He's excited for the next practice where he'll continue to refine his skills. Marco's focus is on growth, progress, and continued improvement.

Let's examine an academic situation next:

Tess is excited to show her aunt her report card after the first term of third grade. "Wow, Tess!" her aunt exclaims, "All 'A's! You are so intelligent, just like your mom!" Tess beams and thinks to herself that it is awesome to be so smart.

What messages did Tess hear from her aunt's "person praise?"
✦ Tess earned straight 'A's because she is intelligent.
✦ Tess's mom is intelligent, so Tess must have been born that way.

Tess's aunt just reinforced a fixed mindset perspective, didn't she? By praising Tess for being smart, she has implied that intelligence is something that you *have* or you *don't have,* not something that you can develop. Tess may now attribute her success in school to the fact that she was born smart. The outcomes of this mindset may be that Tess shies away from more challenging tasks, not wanting to change anyone's mind about her natural intelligence. She might assume that all learning will come easy to her, so when faced with a challenge, she will feel defeated rather than persevere.

How would these situations be different if Marco and Tess were showing signs of failure and not being successful? Researchers Yvonne Skipper and Karen Douglas (2012) at the University of Kent in the United Kingdom found that when children began to fail at a task, using "person praise" led to a negative response to failure far more often than when feedback was given in process terms. Their findings support our belief that praise must be specific in nature and less directed at things that the child cannot change.

Let's consider a different scenario to examine this idea further.

Elise is a 13-year-old who has participated in the recreation center's afterschool art club since kindergarten. Several pieces of Elise's art hang on the walls of the community center, and she won a sculpture contest at her school last fall. She has enjoyed art club for a long time and looks forward to Wednesday afternoons when she can practice her skills and learn new techniques. This year, advanced art club students have access to weekly painting classes with Kesra, an accomplished artist. Kesra has just introduced Elise's group to a new medium, gouache, which is a specialty opaque watercolor. Despite several weeks of practice, Elise is still struggling with the process of color blending and has abandoned several partially completed pieces because she has become frustrated and is unsatisfied with the outcome. Recently, Elise's father has noticed a decline in the amount of time that Elise is spending to prepare for her weekly art club sessions.

"I'm sick of working on this and having it turn out wrong over and over again!" Elise exclaims, emerging from her room with a paintbrush in one hand and a wadded-up piece of art paper in the other. Elise's father cringes—another wasted sheet from the expensive art tablet he gave her for her birthday.

Unsure what to say to his frustrated daughter, Elise's father replies, "Elise, honey, you have a God-given talent for art. Every painting you have ever done is beautiful."

What did Elise hear?
+ She was born with artistic talent.
+ Her dad just wants her to feel better so he says that everything she does is perfect in his eyes.
+ Gouache should come easily for her, just like other techniques.
+ If it doesn't, it might mean that she isn't as good at art as everyone thinks.

Elise's dad chose to use praise to try to reassure his frustrated daughter. He hoped that by reminding her of her talent for art, he would boost her confidence, but in reality, the comment may actually have the opposite effect. Everything that Elise heard contributes to fixed mindset thinking. She was praised for being "natural," rather than for putting forth effort, using strategies, or showing perseverance.

We overhear praise just like that directed to Marco, Tess, and Elise every day. The adults who dole it out do it with good intentions. We (Mary Cay and Meg) do it ourselves! Even after years of studying about, writing about, and making presentations about fixed and growth mindsets, we both still catch ourselves occasionally almost praising children in our lives for being "smart" or "naturally talented." The good news is that (in most cases) we catch ourselves before we say it out loud. We are able to redirect and replace that fixed mindset praise and have added new ways of praise to our repertoire that promote a growth mindset. You can, too—with practice. Let's look at three types of growth mindset praise.

GROWTH MINDSET PRAISE
TYPE 1: EFFORT PRAISE

Embracing challenges with hard work and effort is a hallmark of a growth mindset.

In a fixed mindset, people often view having to work hard as a sign that they are not innately "smart enough" or "talented enough" to do something. This can lead people to give up too early, feel defeated, and assume that they are never going to be good at a particular skill. In a growth mindset, people view hard work and effort as a key to success. We want to be sure that our children understand that having to work hard is not a sign of weakness, but is something that should be embraced! Having to work hard—whether on a math problem, an oil painting, or a new dance routine—helps children to make stronger neural connections and "grow" their brains! Instead of shying away from circumstances that force them to give their best, we want to encourage them to seek out challenges that will require effort. Winston Churchill famously once said, "A pessimist sees the difficulty in every opportunity; an optimist sees the opportunity in every difficulty." Embracing challenges with hard work and effort is a hallmark of a growth mindset.

To develop this quality, we need to ensure that children hear praise connected to effort. Effort praise provides specific feedback that recognizes the hard work that the child is engaged in. For instance:

+ "I can see how hard you are working! Keep it up!"
+ "This isn't easy, is it? That's okay! You're pushing ahead and doing your best!"
+ "I love to see the effort that you put into this project! You must be very proud of it!"
+ "You've been working hard on that for an hour! Good job. How about a break for a snack before you get back at it?"
+ "Even though you don't have the hang of it quite yet, you are so much closer than when you started! I can really see how your determination is paying off!"

> *When children are praised for effort, it is likely*
> *that they will learn a key life lesson earlier*
> *than many of us did: that most everything*
> *worth having in life is born of hard work.*

+ "I know that it is hard to spend so much time on a project like this, but you are going to have a great sense of satisfaction at the end!"
+ "Watching you try different ways to solve that problem reminds me of what I do at work when I am facing a complex situation."

When children are praised for effort, it is likely that they will learn a key life lesson earlier than many of us did: that most everything worth having in life is born of hard work. By viewing having to work hard at something as a positive thing rather than a negative one, children are more likely to seek out challenge and embrace struggle.

GROWTH MINDSET PRAISE TYPE 2: STRATEGY PRAISE

Strategy praise allows us to combine the "feel good" quality of praise with the specificity that adds value to feedback. In strategy praise, we point out to the child that using particular skills and prior knowledge go a long way toward meeting success. Let's consider a scenario in which strategy praise might be appropriate:

Maria's son Thomas is home from college for a mid-semester weekend. He has adjusted well to the academic demands and social opportunities of college life, but is frustrated with his progress in a philosophy course. "The professor is confusing and doesn't seem to like anything I turn in," Thomas lamented over dinner. "I started off thinking that philosophy was going to be an interesting course, but this is just one frustration after another. I've visited the professor during office hours and I've joined the study group she recommended. I hope that helps."

It would be easy for Thomas's mom, Maria, to simply sympathize with Thomas or share that she, too, struggled with similar courses when she was in college. Instead, this is a perfect time to help reinforce a growth mindset by praising the fact that he has already employed several strategies to persevere through the difficult course:

"I'm impressed that you sought out the professor's guidance and joined a study group already," said Maria. "That shows a lot of interest and effort on your part. Good work."

When we use strategy praise, we give children feedback and guidance while also reinforcing that they have made good choices. This combination is important—the feedback component provides several important purposes, according to author and educator Maja Wilson (2012). First, it helps the child improve the final outcome or product. It also supports the child to develop a healthy view of himself or herself as a learner. Finally, it helps the child to develop an understanding of what it means to do the task well.

Researchers at the University of Chicago and Stanford University (Gunderson et al., 2013) undertook an interesting collaborative project in which they measured parents' praise when their children were 2 to 4-years-old to see whether the type of praise the children heard at home in those formative years would affect their performance 5 years later. Interestingly, children who received a lot of praise as toddlers for how they attacked a challenge (rather than just being smart or talented) were far more likely at ages 7 to 9 to select challenging tasks, attribute success and failure to amount of effort, and generate strategies for improvement.

One way to remember to use strategy praise is to shift the focus of our praise. Instead of highlighting the result of the child's work, we can highlight the steps he or she took along the way. Through this lens, we "pay less attention to the end product—the 'A' on the science test, the goal she scored, the 'amazing' painting—and focus on the process it took to get that" (Suissa, 2013, p. 3). Valuable feedback, in the context of strategy praise, helps children to learn and improve while simultaneously fostering a growth mindset.

GROWTH MINDSET PRAISE
TYPE 3: PERSISTENCE PRAISE

Sometimes, despite a heaping dose of hard work and the application of a variety of strategies, we face challenges that require *time* to overcome. Often, these challenges center around new learning, when our brains have to make new connections and "wire themselves" to do something differently. Lack of progress, in the initial stages of learning, can be frustrating to say the least. In order to exhibit persistence, the task also needs to be sufficiently challenging. According to Kristen DiCerbo (2014), who studied children's persistence in game-related learning tasks, "easy tasks will not provide the challenge and failure that will allow for the exhibition of persistence" (p. 20).

Learning to type is a good example that many of us can relate to. Lots of us have jobs that require us to be able to do more than "hunt and peck" on the keyboard, but learning to type is a skill that requires more than just knowledge of the keys and their functions and a commitment to work hard. Along the way, we make many errors. When some of us learned to type, correcting errors required painted-on correction fluid and special reverse keystrokes—thank goodness, all we need to do today is use the backspace key!

Typing, like learning to ride a bike, is a skill that becomes automatic, but only after a great deal of practice. Practice takes time. If we had grown frustrated and given up without putting forth enough time, we would not have become proficient typists.

This leads to the third type of growth mindset-oriented praise—persistence praise. When we praise children for pushing through the frustration, we help them to recognize that sometimes tasks require us to put forth effort *over a long period of time*. Many children become easily discouraged when they are not able to solve a puzzle, execute a front handspring, master long division, or sink a foul shot. In the book *NurtureShock: Why Everything We Think About Raising Our Children Is Wrong*, authors Po Bronson and Ashley Merryman (2009) found that just as mice can be trained to overcome frustration when finding food in a maze, the (human) brain has to learn to persevere through challenges.

> *When we praise children for pushing through the frustration, we help them to recognize that sometimes tasks require us to put forth effort over a long period of time.*

Many skills take time to perfect, but a child's concept of time is very different from ours. Just ask a -year-old to wait 10 minutes for something, and you will see what we mean. For this reason, persistence praise reinforces the notion that it is normal for some things to take time to develop. Let's look at how this can be used:

Angela is a 10-year-old who joined the neighborhood swim team for the first time. The coach placed her in the 25-meter freestyle event for her first meet, hoping that she would gain confidence from a short distance and a simple stroke. Angela was nervous, but started off the blocks with her goggles firmly in place and swimming furiously. Her parents watched Angela from the side of the pool, helpless as they saw her swimming toward the lane line and beginning to struggle. Angela's coach was watching, too, and cheered her on.

Angela could tell that the other children had already finished the race when she was just halfway down the pool. Her parents saw her look around and wondered if she would stop swimming and give up. But Angela tucked her head down and kicked as hard as she could, zigzagging her way down the lane, until she finally reached the wall.

"Wow, Angela! Good swim!" her coach said. "I could see that you were having some trouble with the lane line, but you didn't let it throw you off. You didn't give up!"

The persistence praise that Angela's coach used both acknowledged the challenge she felt and reinforced her decision to push through it. Angela will most certainly encounter other races in which she will lose her goggles, mess up a turn, or finish last. By using persistence praise, her coach has taught her to view these challenges as surmountable.

THE POWER OF YET

The praise examples we have shared so far leave little doubt as to the power of our words to influence how children make decisions about next steps. With deliberate thought and practice, you can adopt growth mindset praise on a regular basis. But there is one more language tip that we think may be the most useful of all over the long haul.

We've all heard adults say to children, "Say the magic word!" when they want to cue the child to say "please" when requesting a cookie, a toy, or an extra helping of Brussels sprouts (okay, well maybe not the last one). No one can argue that "please" is not a very important word and concept for children to use and understand, but when cultivating a growth mindset, there is also a "magic word." That magic word is *yet.*

Yet is a hopeful word that means "at a future time." It has powerful implications for building a growth mindset because it is the antidote for the fixed view of "I can't." Just because a child can't do something at the moment doesn't mean it will never be accomplished. Imagine how many things would never have been discovered, how many records would never have been broken, and how many dreams would never have been realized if people had lived in the world of "I can't." Not being able to make that breakthrough, solve the problem, or play the instrument flawlessly *today* is temporary. With hard work, effort, and increased skill, improvement and accomplishment are always possible. Therein lies the power of *yet*.

Hearing the word "yet" is especially powerful when children are given feedback from adults about a skill that they have not mastered. In a 2017 study, Haimovitz and Dweck looked at the words that parents and teachers used after students received a failing grade on a writing assignment. Children who heard the word "yet" as part of the feedback reported feeling more encouraged and motivated than those who did not. The researchers called this a "failure-is-enhancing" mindset, meaning that making multiple attempts at something often makes the end result stronger! As noted in the paper summarizing their research, "Parents who saw failure as enhancing were more likely to respond with a focus on the process of learning" (Haimovitz & Dweck, 2017).

> Yet *is a hopeful word that means "at a future time." It has powerful implications for building a growth mindset because it is the antidote for the fixed view of "I can't."*

Maybe you will be able to relate to this scenario:

Rosa is a childcare provider who looks after four preschool-aged children during the day while their parents are at work. In addition to interactive play and healthy meals, Rosa ensures that the children have time to practice their alphabet and numbers. Three-year-old Alexandra is struggling mightily with learning how to write her name. "I have too many letters!" she exclaims. "I can't do it!" Alexandra quickly dissolves into a bundle of sobs after seeing that the other three children have accomplished the name-writing task. Rosa attempts to calm Alexandra down and helps her to finish writing her name, but secretly wishes she used the nickname "Alex" or "Ali" so that they could avoid this all-too-familiar meltdown.

Will Alexandra master the writing of her name? Sure, she will! Will it happen overnight? Probably not! Writing your name is a complicated endeavor that takes learning the order of the letters and then learning how to make each one. Just like Alexandra won't be able to hop on a bicycle and ride, she needs time to practice how to write her name. She can't do it *yet*. Rosa could reinforce this idea by using the word *yet* in her conversations with Alexandra. The next time Alexandra says, "I can't!" or "I don't know how!" Rosa can respond with, "Maybe you can't *yet*, but with some more practice, you will be able to do it!"

It isn't just preschoolers who fall into the "I can't" trap. We all do! It is a trap because it typically stops forward momentum toward a goal. When children declare that they can't do something, or they aren't good enough, or they don't know how, they are off the hook to accomplish that task. They can "opt out" of hard work or further effort because they have declared something too challenging.

At Monocacy Middle School in Frederick, MD, former principal Brian Vasquenza and his staff did something very simple, but powerful, when they printed *YET* in large black letters on bright yellow paper and hung it in every room in their school. Vasquenza and his teachers wanted to impact the culture of the school so that students were not permitted to "opt out" of challenging work or rigorous learning. Seeing the word reminded the students and the adults in the building that they are learning, growing, and improving every day. When a student started to say, "I can't," teachers just pointed to the word. Students began using the word *yet* to encourage each other. The power of the magic word *yet* reminded everyone that learning new things is challenging, no one is expected to be an expert immediately, and with dedication and hard work, success follows.

> When children declare that they can't do something, or they aren't good enough, or they don't know how, they are off the hook to accomplish that task. They can "opt out" of hard work or further effort because they have declared something too challenging.

Even Sesame Street embraced the idea of using the word *yet* when singer Janelle Monae visited the show in its 45th season. Janelle and the characters sing and dance while teaching children that success takes time. This video can be viewed at www.youtube.com/watch?v= XLeUvZvuvAs.

For the older kids, check out C. J. Luckey, a hip-hop artist who wrote and created a music video, *The Power of Yet*. This video can be found at www.youtube.com/watch?v=J6CnrFvY94E.

PRACTICING GROWTH MINDSET PRAISE AND FEEDBACK

We had the good fortune to meet fellow Marylander Jack Andraka when he was 16 and determined to find a cure for pancreatic cancer. By the time he was 18, Jack was a scientist, inventor, cancer researcher, Stanford University freshman, and author—an impressive resume for anyone. (You might be wondering why HIS parents haven't written a parenting book!) Jack's parents, Steve and Jane, raised two independent, innovative thinkers. When writer Seth Stevenson (2015) of *The Wall Street Journal* asked them to share advice with other parents, Jane said, "Don't just tell your kids how smart they are. Praise your kids' effort and persistence. Tell them that failure is fine and that you like the way they work through things" (para. 16).

This deliberate message was pivotal in developing Jack's determination and drive. After becoming interested in early warning signs of pancreatic cancer at age 14, Jack came up with an idea for a simple, rapid-response test that he hoped could detect pancreatic cancer early enough to provide time for medical intervention. He sent his scientific proposal to 200 different professors who were involved in pancreatic cancer research:

> Dear Dr. So-and-So,
>
> I am a high school student who attends North County High School. I am currently doing a science fair project on the use of nanotubes and antibodies to detect pancreatic cancer (strain RIP1). For my project, I plan on producing my antigens and antibodies through the immunization of mice with MUC1. The MUC1 will be derived from xenografted RIP1 in mice and will be extracted using a hot phenol: water extraction procedure. My procedure is attached to this email. I was wondering if I could work in your laboratory to produce MUC1, which will then be used to produce PAM4. Thank you for your time, your research is absolutely amazing. If you cannot help me can you refer me to someone who can.
>
> Sincerely, Jack Andraka
> (Andraka, 2015, p. 116)

Jack attached a 30-page detailed proposal to his request. And no, you are not alone—we have no idea what MUC1s are either! Jack's expertise in this area and understanding of cancer research far exceeds our understanding. But the fact remains that over the next few weeks, rejection after rejection flowed in. Jack's mindset, and that of his parents, was severely tested. The 193rd response to Jack's inquiry for help came from Dr. Anirban Maitra of Johns Hopkins University, who allowed Jack to use his lab to work on the project, which went on to win the 2012 Intel Science and Engineering Competition and continues to hold promise for future rapid diagnosis for several types of cancer (Andraka, 2015).

REPLACING PARENTS' FIXED MINDSET STATEMENTS

Read each of the fixed mindset statements that you, as a parent, might say about yourself in the left column. Write at least one growth mindset statement that could replace the fixed mindset statement. The first one is an example.

FIXED MINDSET STATEMENT	GROWTH MINDSET REPLACEMENT STATEMENT
I am a terrible cook!	*I need to find some videos online that demonstrate some of these cooking techniques that I can't do yet.*
I will never be good at that.	
I have a green thumb.	
I leave that (finance, technology, cooking, etc.) to my partner.	
You can't teach an old dog new tricks.	

FIGURE 3.1 PARENT REPLACEMENT STATEMENTS

REPLACING PARENT TO CHILD FIXED MINDSET STATEMENTS

Read each of the fixed mindset statements that you, as a parent, might say in the left column. Write at least one growth mindset statement that could replace the fixed mindset statement. The first one is an example.

FIXED MINDSET STATEMENT	GROWTH MINDSET REPLACEMENT STATEMENT
You are so smart!	*I can see how much effort you put into your work!*
You are "gifted." You should know how to do this.	
Math wasn't my thing either.	
None of us in this family are good at _____.	
You are so lucky; you don't have to study much!	
You are my little artist and your sister is my little author.	
This is so easy for you. You don't even have to try!	

FIGURE 3.2 PARENT TO CHILD REPLACEMENT STATEMENTS

How would this story have been different if Jane and Steve Andraka had not adopted a growth mindset view of praise and feedback? Would Jack have been able to persevere through disappointment to move closer and closer to the fulfillment of his dream? Jack doesn't miss a chance to credit his parents with helping him to learn to push on through challenges. Who better to be leading the next generation of cancer researchers than someone with a growth mindset like Jack?

Adopting growth mindset praise and feedback in our homes is not as easy as you may think. It takes practice, time, and growth mindset thinking from parents, guardians, and especially grandparents! Figure 3.1 provides an opportunity to think how you could replace your own fixed mindset statements with growth mindset statements. Figure 3.2 helps you to replace some common fixed mindset statements that parents direct to their children with growth mindset statements. If you are reading this book as part of a book club or with a partner, discuss each statement together and come up with as many replacement growth mindset statements as you can. (If you need to, you can peek at some suggested replacement statements that can be found in Appendix B.) As you come up with growth mindset statements, ask yourself the following:

- ✦ Does the replacement statement provide specific feedback?
- ✦ Does the replacement statement focus on the process the child is engaged in rather than the person?
- ✦ Does the replacement statement reinforce the value you place on effort, hard work, and overcoming obstacles or challenges?

REFERENCES

Andraka, J. (2015). *Breakthrough: How one teen innovator is changing the world.* New York, NY: Harper.

Bronson, P., & Merryman, A. (2009). *NutureShock: New thinking about children.* New York, NY: Twelve.

DiCerbo, K. (2014). Game-based assessment of persistence. *Educational Technology & Society, 17*, 17–28.

Dweck, C. (2006). *Mindset: The new psychology of success.* New York, NY: Random House.

Gunderson, E. Griphover, S., Romero, C., Dweck, C., Goldin-Meadow, S. & Levine, S. (2013). Parent praise to 1- to 3-year olds predicts children's motivational frameworks 5 years later. *Child Development, 84*, 1526–1541.

Haimovitz, K., & Dweck, C. S. (2017). The origins of children's growth and fixed mindsets: New research and a new proposal. *Child Development, 88*(6), 1849–1859. https://doi.org/10.1111/cdev.12955

Skipper, Y. & Douglas, K. (2012). Is no praise good praise? Effects of positive feedback on children's and university students' responses to subsequent failures. *British Journal of Educational Psychology, 82*, 327–339.

Stevenson, S. (2015). Jack Andraka's parents on raising a science whiz kid. *The Wall Street Journal.* Retrieved April 10, 2023 from www.wsj.com/articles/jack-andrakas-parents-on-raising-a-science-whiz-kid-1446562556.

Suissa, J. (2013). Tiger mothers and praise junkies: Children, praise, and the reactive attitudes. *Journal of Philosophy of Education, 47*(1), 1–19.

Wilson, M. (2012). What do we do when a child says … "Look at my drawing!" *Educational Leadership, 70*(1), 52–56.

CHAPTER 4

WHY IS IT IMPORTANT FOR CHILDREN TO UNDERSTAND HOW THE BRAIN WORKS?

"When I practice my numbers, I can feel my neurons connecting."
—Olivia, age 5

As educators, we have spent countless hours over the past several years sharing the power of growth mindsets with students, teachers, school administrators, and parents. We try to help those various audiences walk away from our sessions with a solid overall understanding of the research about mindset and the implications it has in their particular area of interest. Teachers are often the most challenging audiences—and for good reason. They have participated in countless professional learning sessions and have seen many trends in education come and go. Some of what they have learned has resonated with them and made positive impacts on the achievement of their students, and other sessions have done little to affect their day-to-day teaching lives. For this reason, they might enter our professional learning session with a healthy dose of skepticism. They want to know what "science" backs up our information about mindsets. Teenagers often share the same skepticism, particularly when they hear adults saying, "Keep persevering! Have a growth mindset!" We welcome their skepticism and are happy to talk to them about the brain science behind growth and fixed mindsets.

Teachers have a new field of study about the brain to understand and benefit from that didn't exist when the two of us started our classroom careers. Called "the science of learning," or "cognitive neuroscience," or "mind, brain, and education science," these titles refer to a combining of the fields of study about the brain, how it learns, and how we should go about teaching as a result. Just like many other advances as the result of technology, the ways that scientists can "see" inside the learning brain through the use of imaging has made this field grow by leaps and bounds in the last few decades. Our work has been greatly influenced by our learning about how the brain learns, grows, and thrives. It has confirmed a lot of what we knew about learning from watching our own children and students, and it has opened our eyes to new ways to help the learning brain. We hope that this field continues to grow in the coming years. It is only fitting that all of us—whether parents, teachers, coaches, or adults who support children in a variety of other ways—should know the best ways to support the development of the central organ of learning, the brain.

It is important for all of us to have a basic understanding of how the brain "grows" in its connections and the power of neuroplasticity. Do not worry—this chapter won't cause you to break out in a sweat! Come with us on a fantastic journey about the body's most fascinating organ.

NEUROSCIENCE 101

Our brains may seem like small organs, but size is deceptive! The human brain has two halves, called hemispheres. Each hemisphere consists of brain tissue that is folded in complex ways. If unfolded, each hemisphere of the human brain might stretch to the size of an extra-large pizza. That is a lot of room for learning!

> *When neurons connect, a synapse occurs. These connections are strengthened with practice and effort.*

In its simplest form, learning is a process of forming or modifying connections (called synapses) among brain cells (neurons). Humans have, on average, 86 billion neurons (Herculano-Houzel, 2016). All these neurons spend their time making connections that help us to process information that we take in through our various senses. When neurons connect, a synapse occurs. These connections are strengthened with practice and effort. The more connections, the denser your brain is.

Picture brand-new learning experiences as neurons being connected by a thin piece of thread. Every time new learning is practiced and applied, that thin thread becomes stronger and stronger until the learning is mastered. By now, that weak, thin piece of thread has the strength of a thick, strong rope. Prior knowledge and experiences help these connections to strengthen. The more connections that are made during learning, the more physical changes occur in the brain by developing and strengthening neural pathways.

A new neural pathway is like walking through an unexplored forest for the first time. The more frequently the path is used, the fewer the obstacles and barriers that stand in the way. Eventually a clear path is created. That new path represents a clear understanding of the concept being taught (Ricci, 2018). When the pathway is no longer used (perhaps due to a summer without reading), the connection can weaken and become thin again. Because the connection was once strong, after review and practice the connection will strengthen again. This is one reason the first week of a new school year is often a review of the past year's learning targets.

Science used to tell us that as we age, we lose brain cells (neurons). Not so! We keep those brain cells. What happens instead is that the connections might weaken, which is why it is important to keep our elderly family members and friends both physically and cognitively active.

NEUROPLASTICITY

When we examine the word *neuroplasticity*, we see two familiar terms: *neuro*, meaning brain, and *plasticity*, meaning changeability. Neuroplasticity describes the flexibility and changeability of the brain. These changes happen when neurons connect, when those connections get stronger, and when those connections get weaker. Over the last few decades, technology has enabled scientists and medical professionals to use special imaging systems to view these neural connections. These researchers describe the changes seen in the human brain over time—changes that happen through new learning, focused practice, and deliberate effort. Science provides the key to explaining that our brains are dynamic organs that have the capability to grow and change!

> Neuroplasticity is the key to the brain's ability to adapt to new ways of doing things.

Let's consider a quick example of neuroplasticity. Imagine that you come home to find that someone has reorganized your kitchen cabinets. (For some of us this might be a blessing, but for others it would be a nightmare!) When you open the cabinet over the toaster expecting to find your plates, bowls, and glasses, instead you find cereal, crackers, soup, and pasta. More investigating reveals that your dishes are now in the cabinet closest to the dishwasher. Although the new arrangement is logical, it is likely to cause you frustration! For the first several days, you will reach for a bowl and end up with a box of pasta. You'll look for cereal and instead see plates. Think about how many times you operated under the "old" kitchen arrangement. That was a lot of practice for your brain. The neural connections related to locating things in your kitchen were very strong, likely automatic most of the time. When a change is made, the brain has to create a new neural connection with the new locations while slowly trying to extinguish the tight grip on the strong neural connections related to the old way of doing things. The good news is that the brain has the capacity to learn new ways of doing things, even when the old ways are ingrained. Yes, you can "teach an old dog new tricks!" Neuroplasticity is the key to the brain's ability to adapt to new ways of doing things. In a few short weeks, it is likely that your brain will have adapted to the new cupboard organization and you will not find yourself eating dinner on a box of crackers instead of a plate!

On a larger scale, the brain's neuroplasticity also allows it to recover from trauma. When a person suffers a brain injury, such as a stroke, neural connections are often broken. If the part of the brain with the broken connection recovers from the stroke, new connections can be formed with practice and repetition. There are even instances where people have had to have entire hemispheres of their brains removed and neuroplasticity enables the opposite hemisphere to make new neural connections to make up for many that were lost.

Why is this brain science important? Because children need a working knowledge of the most sophisticated organ in their bodies. Increase of motivation, willingness to accept new challenges, and healthier reaction to failure are only a few of the benefits children will experience when they understand how their brains work (Ricci, 2018). We want children to be able to visualize neurons connecting when they are learning new skills. We want them to imagine their neural connections getting thicker and stronger when they persevere through a challenging assignment. We want them to approach tasks with the knowledge that their brains are capable of growing and that they are capable of getting "smarter." For many children, being able to harness the power of this information is truly a game-changer.

> *Increase of motivation, willingness to accept new challenges, and healthier reaction to failure are only a few of the benefits children will experience when they understand how their brains work (Ricci, 2018).*

INCREASE MOTIVATION? DECREASE FRUSTRATION? YES, PLEASE!

Carol Dweck and fellow Stanford researcher Kali Trzesniewski teamed up with Lisa Blackwell of Columbia University in 2007 to examine whether students' mindsets influenced their academic achievement at a key transitional period in their adolescence. They chose seventh-grade mathematics as the focus of their study because middle school often brings with it less support than students may have received in elementary years, along with math concepts of increasing complexity and abstraction. (If you are a parent of an adolescent, you can share stories of frustrations and meltdowns during this period as well!) Blackwell, Trzesniewski, and Dweck (2007) found that students with a growth mindset toward learning math (measured using a survey) outperformed the more fixed mindset students over the course of the year. More interesting for our discussion about brain science, they found that children's focus on the ability of their brains to grow and change (neuroplasticity) was a considerable influence on their mindset, and ultimately, their motivation.

> Helping kids to understand that the struggles we experience when we are learning new and challenging things are normal and are actually a sign of our neural connections strengthening is a powerful way to transform their attitude and their perspective.

We know that some of the most trying situations for parents happen when children come home from school frustrated and grumbling about an academic struggle. Often, the source of the problem is unclear, the child grows more anxious or angry with each passing day of the class, and we, as adults, find ourselves unsure if the source of the problem lies with the teacher, the child, or a combination of both. Children facing academic struggles may assume they are "not smart enough" to manage the work, disengage from the classroom activities, and announce that they "hate school" or "hate [fill-in-your-choice-of-subject]." Helping kids to understand that the struggles we experience when we are learning new and challenging things are normal and are a sign of our neural connections strengthening is a powerful way to transform their attitude and their perspective. Let's examine some practical ways we can help children understand the "science" behind struggle.

THE POWER OF LANGUAGE

When we talked about praise and feedback in chapter 3, we examined how influential and significant words can be in sending messages about what we value. The same is true when it comes to basic brain science. If we deliberately use a few key terms when we talk to children about learning and persevering, we will send powerful messages about a growth mindset orientation.

Research has shown that young children hear very few instances of the word *brain* in everyday conversation (Corriveau, Pasquini, & Harris, 2005). How many phrases can you think of that include the word brain? The closest that some children hear adults say is, "Make up your mind," or "Wear a helmet to protect your noggin." Even through the early elementary years, most children view the brain as a "container" for thoughts, memories, and preferences, but do not really understand its basic workings or its power to change and get stronger (Dalton & Bergenn, 2007). Let's see this in action:

Imagine that 8-year-old Henry is working on a challenging math homework assignment. He is becoming frustrated with the many steps involved in solving the math problem and is angry at himself that he has failed to solve the problem on which he is working. He is about to resort to pencil smashing when his older brother, Charlie, sits down at the kitchen table with him.

"Wow, Henry, you have been working on these problems for a long time. I can see how much effort you have put into this." (His brother knows something about growth mindset praise, doesn't he?)

"But it is still wrong!" Henry exclaims. "I am so tired of all these steps. If you forget even one step the whole thing is wrong. I hate this!"

"Your brain is learning something new, Henry. Part of the process is that you will make some mistakes and get frustrated. It's just like when you are at soccer practice and you have to keep running even though you are tired. Each time you do, your legs get stronger. Every time you keep trying at math, you are growing new connections in your brain that will get stronger and stronger as you learn how to do long division. Let's look at that problem again."

As Henry starts to tackle the problem one more time with Charlie's support, he has a new perspective on the struggle. By talking about his brain and the connections that are being formed, Charlie related Henry's frustration about long division to things that Henry already knows. Just as his legs might get tired and ache a bit as he is building strong muscles at soccer practice, his brain is "tired and achy" as it is learning new things, too. But just as his legs are stronger after he trains, his brain is stronger after he struggles, too. He has also heard the message that struggle is normal and is part of the learning process when we are accomplishing hard things.

When we visit classrooms where teachers share basic neuroscience with children, it is always a wonderful experience. In these classrooms, children have learned about neurons and the brain's ability to grow new connections and strengthen old ones. Hearing so many insightful and humorous comments from kids as we visit classrooms is heart-warming—everything from, "I can FEEL my brain growing!" to "I am ready for a challenge, so my neurons stretch out and connect!"

A favorite was from a kindergartener who understood the concept of neuroplasticity but was struggling with the scientific terminology: "My 'nerds' (neurons) are connecting, and it is making my brain smarter!" We also enjoyed the time a third-grade student exclaimed, "So this is why my head hurts when I think too much!"

> By using just a few simple words in everyday conversation, we can make the brain's role more understood, relevant, and powerful to our children.

A parent recently related a story about her kindergarten daughter, who had learned at school that when we do not give up, but keep trying, our neural connections strengthen. She had also learned that if we do not use our neural connections, they can weaken. Early one Saturday morning, the little girl's father awoke to find her sleeping on the floor in her parents' bedroom. When he asked her for a reason that she was not in her own bed in her own room, the kindergartener had a lengthy list of excuses. Her dad replied, "You should just give up!" meaning that her silly reasons did not make any sense. The child replied, "I can't give up! If I do, my neurons will stop connecting!"

It is exciting to hear children use the words *brain, neuron,* and *connection* because by talking about the brain and what it can do, children show that they have some ownership over a part of their bodies that is otherwise fairly mysterious. Because children can't see their own brains, they rely on others to talk about them. By using just a few simple words in everyday conversation, we can make the brain's role better understood, relevant, and powerful to our children.

One of the best ways to ensure that children understand how the brain works and how it can grow as they learn new things is through everyday interactions. Figure 4.1, brain-focused feedback, presents some common scenarios and ideas for how to respond or provide feedback using brain-focused language.

BRAIN-FOCUSED FEEDBACK

SCENARIO	BRAIN-FOCUSED FEEDBACK
Your child becomes frustrated because she can't hit the softball while playing in the backyard.	"We all have to practice skills that are new and challenging for us. Your brain is strengthening neural connections every time you work on batting. Keep trying."
Your toddler is focused and intent on inserting shapes into the proper slots on the sorting toy.	"Your brain is really working at that! Good job!"
Your teenager is studying for tomorrow's science test.	"Looks like your brain is really getting a workout! You're making lots of neural connections about science tonight."
Your high school student wants to quit the school play after seeing how many lines he has to memorize.	"That's going to stretch your brain, but you can do it. Your brain can strengthen its ability to memorize. I'll help you practice."
Your child comes home with a worksheet and needs to correct the errors for homework. She says, "This is a waste of time."	"Correcting mistakes helps you grow. We can rewire our brains just by practicing the skill the right way. Making those corrections is valuable."
Your college student says that being a biology major is too hard and says, "I'm not smart enough for this!"	"Don't give up before you give your brain a chance to adjust to the level of work you're being asked to do. With every hour that you study, you are strengthening neural connections and deepening your understanding of what you are learning."

FIGURE 4.1 BRAIN-FOCUSED FEEDBACK

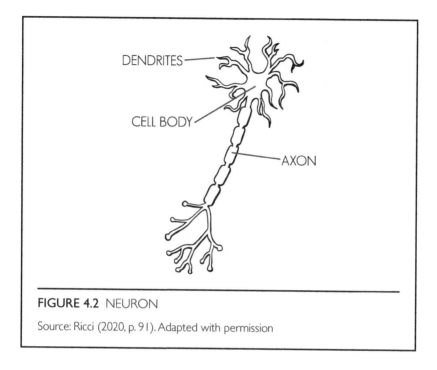

FIGURE 4.2 NEURON

Source: Ricci (2020, p. 91). Adapted with permission

VISUALIZE NEURONS AND NEURAL CONNECTIONS

Recent studies estimate that the average human has 86,060,000,000 neurons (Harrigan & Commons, 2014)! There are 86,400 seconds in a day, so if you *could* count your neurons one by one, you would need to count more than a million neurons per second to finish counting in 24 hours. (That is an example that will make your head itch from the neurons connecting!) Helping to make an abstract "thing" like a neuron real to children is a challenge, but we believe that it is an important part of helping them to learn about the brain and the power of neurons to connect with new learning.

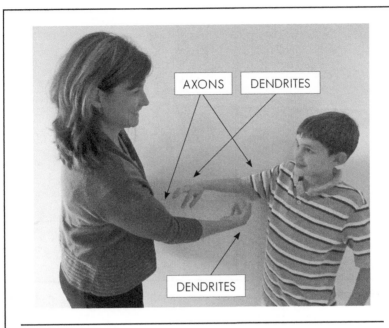

FIGURE 4.3 DEMONSTRATING A NEURAL CONNECTION

Neurons, in their simplest form, consist of a few parts, as shown in Figure 4.2. The simplest way to make a neuron is with your own hand and arm (see Figure 4.3). Dr. Marcia Tate, distinguished educator and author from Georgia, shares this way of visualizing a neuron with educators when she lectures, and it is a great way to teach children as well. Your palm is the cell body, your arm is the axon, and your fingers and thumb are dendrites. If you would like to make a connection with another neuron, just remember that dendrites do not connect with other dendrites—dendrites connect with axons.

Once you know the three basic parts of a neuron, you can get creative with how to make them. We have seen great pipe cleaner neurons, neurons made from play dough or putty, drawn with markers, or even made out of food. Kids love to be creative about expressing their understanding of what neurons look like, and it is even more fun when they think about the enormous number of neurons they have inside their own brains. The possibilities are limitless for creating neurons and illustrating how they make connections.

One powerful visual was created by Angela Thomas, a primary talent development teacher in Frederick County, MD. After working with the students during the school year and teaching them about neuroplasticity, Angela wanted to help children keep track of the neural connections that they were building and strengthening over the summer, so she created a simple brain worksheet and asked students to use colored pencils or crayons to record their growing neural connections as they tried something new and/or practiced it. Initial experiences got a simple, thin line, but the line could be colored darker and wider with practice. Angela also asked the children to color-code their learning with a key so that they could keep track of different new experiences in different colors. She used child-friendly language, labeling the connections "new," "try, try again," and "strong." The simple visual reminder, placed on the refrigerator or over the child's desk during the summer months, helped to motivate the children to persevere and take on new challenges. In addition to the brain graphic, the children also kept a list of their activities on the back of the sheet. Not just a powerful visual, this also serves as a fantastic record of growth over time that could be saved and treasured—the child will enjoy returning to look at it year after year.

Another idea for parents is to include conversation about strong and "not yet" neural connections as your child is learning a new skill. If you see your child struggling as she learns a new piano technique, remind her that her neural connection is just beginning—just a very thin connection. As she practices and shows more growth, remind her that those connections are continuing to get stronger, but are not quite there "yet." You can use the worksheets in the next section to help you with this.

BOOKS AND ONLINE RESOURCES ABOUT THE BRAIN

Here are a few resources that you and your children may enjoy as you learn more about the brain. This list includes worksheets (Figures 4.4, 4.5, and 4.6) and other resources that share accurate information about the brain and how it works—an important distinction because some children's books and websites about the brain have taken "creative license" when it comes to neuroscience, sacrificing accuracy for entertainment.

BOOKS FOR CHILDREN

+ *Your Fantastic Elastic Brain: Stretch It, Shape It* by JoAnn Deak (Little Pickle Press, 2010)—This richly illustrated picture book does an excellent job of making neuroscience fun and engaging.
+ *Good Night to Your Fantastic Elastic Brain* by JoAnn Deak and Terrence Deak (Sourcebooks, 2022)—This sequel provides additional information about the brain and how it benefits from sleep in a relatable, entertaining way.
+ *The Owner's Manual for Driving Your Adolescent Brain* by JoAnn Deak and Terrence Deak (Little Pickle Press, 2013)—This book grapples with teenage-specific brain questions while maintaining the same engaging style of their books for younger children.
+ *Neurology for Kids* by Betty Nguyen and Brandon Pham (Black Phoenix Press, 2022)—A simple picture book for ages 6 to 10 written by doctors, this guide includes a good explanation of neural connections and the various parts of the brain.
+ *My First Book About the Brain* by Donald M. Silver and Patricia J. Wynne (Dover Publications, 2013)—This is a coloring book approach, suitable for ages 8 to 12.
+ *How to Be a Genius* (DK Publishing, 2013)—Comprehensive and engaging, this book includes wonderful graphics

to illustrate the work of the brain; we just wish it had a different title!

✦ *The Big Brain Book: How It Works and All Its Quirks* by Leanne Boucher Gill (Magination Press, 2021)—This is a large and comprehensive encyclopedia about the brain and how it works that includes lots of engaging and helpful graphics.

✦ *Battle of the Brains: The Science Behind Animal Minds* by Jocelyn Rish (Running Press Kids, 2022)—Reaching beyond the human brain to investigate the brains of our favorite animals, children will love this book about how animal brains are unique.

✦ *Brain Games: The Mind-Blowing Science of Your Amazing Brain* by Jennifer Swanson (National Geographic Kids, 2015)—This book is filled with fun facts, games, and optical illusions.

✦ *Neurocomic* by Matteo Farinella and Hana Ros (Nobrow Ltd., 2013)—A graphic novel written and illustrated by two neuroscientists, this book is a delight for teenagers and adults.

✦ *The Brain is Kind of a Big Deal* by Nick Seluk (Scholastic, 2019)—A delightful, richly-illustrated and captivating book that gets the brain science right.

✦ *Brain Lab for Kids: 52 Mind-Blowing Experiments, Models, and Activities to Explore Neuroscience* by Eric Chudler (Quarry Books, 2018)—The neuroscientist behind a fantastic monthly e-newsletter for kids and families (referenced below) has created a collection of hands-on ways to learn about the brain that are appropriate for all ages.

✦ *A Parent's Guide to the Science of Learning: 77 Studies That Every Parent Needs to Know* by Edward Watson and Bradley Busch (Routledge, 2022)—This is a concise, easy-to-read book for adults that summarizes many key research studies about learning. The authors (full disclosure: Meg's friends!) use a color-coded, two-page format to let you know exactly what each study means for you and the children you love.

WEBSITES

✦ Dana Alliance for Brain Initiatives (www.dana.org/BAW/ Education)—The Dana Alliance is a private philanthropic foundation that supports brain research. This website is a compilation of resources for children and parents, including an online activity book for elementary-aged students and links to photos, information, brain puzzles, and more.

✦ Neuroscience for Kids (http://faculty.washington.edu/chudler/ neurok.html)—The Neuroscience for Kids website came about because of a Science Education Partnership Award with the University of Washington. Dr. Eric Chudler maintains a robust collection of articles, experiments, contests, and facts just for kids. Dr. Chudler also publishes a fact-filled monthly e-mail newsletter geared to children, their teachers, and their parents.

✦ BrainFacts (www.brainfacts.org)—The Society for Neuroscience helps to maintain BrainFacts.org, a website appropriate for teens and adults. The site includes information about the brain and its functions as well as profiles of current neuroscientists and their research.

_____'S BRAIN

Record your connections as you try new
things or work hard to improve.

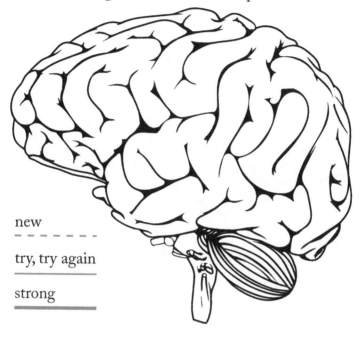

new

try, try again

strong

FIGURE 4.4 BLANK BRAIN WORKSHEET

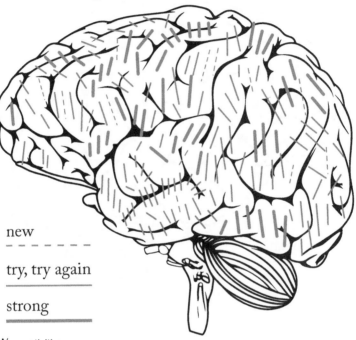

Connor 'S BRAIN

Record your connections as you try new
things or work hard to improve.

new
- - - - - -

try, try again
_____

strong
▬▬▬▬▬▬

New activities:
1. climbing trees
2. being a volunteer in a magic show
3. LEGO robotics
4. making pickles
5. painting pottery
6. card game
7. running with Daddy

Activities that I worked to improve:
1. baseball
2. fishing
3. swimming
4. gardening
5. mini golf
6. basketball
7. catching sandcrabs
8. math
9. writing
10. problem solving
11. reading

FIGURE 4.5 COMPLETED BRAIN WORKSHEET

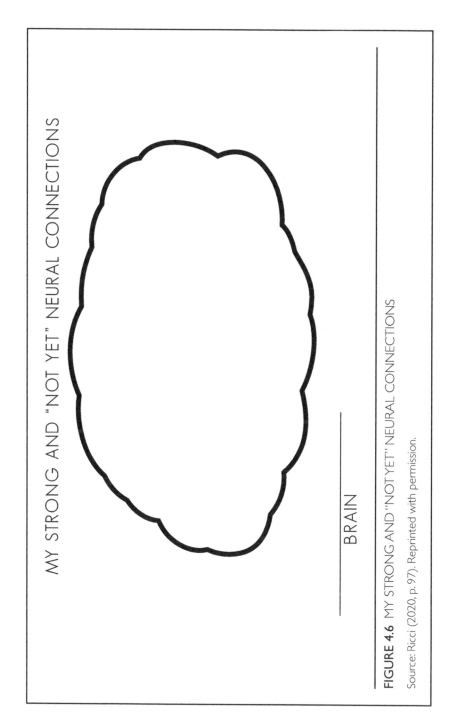

MY STRONG AND "NOT YET" NEURAL CONNECTIONS

BRAIN

FIGURE 4.6 MY STRONG AND "NOT YET" NEURAL CONNECTIONS

Source: Ricci (2020, p. 97). Reprinted with permission.

REFERENCES

Blackwell, L., Trzesniewski, K., & Dweck, C. (2007). Implicit theories of intelligence predict achievement across an adolescent transition: A longitudinal study and an intervention. *Child Development, 78,* 246–263. doi:10.1111/j.1467-8624.2007.00995.x.

Corriveau, K., Pasquini, E., & Harris, P. (2005). If it's in your brain, it's in your mind: Children's developing anatomy of identity. *Cognitive Development, 20,* 321–340.

Dalton, T. & Bergenn, V. (2007). *Early experience, the brain, and consciousness: An historical and interdisciplinary synthesis.* New York, NY: Lawrence Erlbaum.

Harrigan, W., & Commons, M. (2014). The stage of development of a species predicts the number of neurons. *Behavioral Development Bulletin 19*(4), 12–21.

Herculano-Houzel, S. (2016). *The Human Advantage: A New Understanding of How Our Brain Became Remarkable.* Cambridge, MA: The MIT Press.

Ricci, M. (2018). *Mindsets in the classroom: Building a growth mindset learning community* (updated ed.). Waco, TX: Prufrock Press.

Ricci, M. (2020). *Ready-to-use resources for mindsets in the classroom: Everything educators need for school success.* Waco, TX: Prufrock Press.

CHAPTER 5

HOW CAN WE DEVELOP PERSEVERANCE AND RESILIENCY IN OUR CHILDREN?

"I don't give up. I keep trying, because eventually I'll figure it out."

—Morgan, age 14

Before we discuss how to develop perseverance and resiliency, let's first talk about why we should develop these important skills. Many of us are not aware that approximately 75% of achievement is attributed to psychosocial skills (which some researchers refer to as noncognitive factors) and only approximately 25% of innate intelligence or IQ contributes to achievement (Olszewski-Kubilius, 2013). Psychosocial skills are those skills that all our children should cultivate in order to achieve. The cultivation of psychosocial skills is imperative for all of us. These psychosocial skills include, but are not limited to, perseverance, resiliency, grit, determination, and tenacity. These all must be deliberately modeled in the home and purposefully cultivated.

DOI: 10.4324/9781003405931-6

> *Many of us are not aware that approximately 75% of achievement is attributed to psychosocial skills (which some researchers refer to as noncognitive factors) and only approximately 25% of innate intelligence or IQ contributes to achievement.*

According to the U.S. Department of Education (2013) report, *Promoting Grit, Tenacity and Perseverance: Critical Factors for Success in the 21st Century,* certain "factors are essential to an individual's capacity to strive for and succeed at long-term and high-order goals, and to persist in the face of the array of challenges and obstacles encountered throughout schooling and life" (p. v). The report goes on to state that our children can develop the resources needed to persevere by being aware of these three things:

✦ *Academic mindsets:* How we frame ourselves as learners. As the report stated:

Compelling evidence suggests that mindsets can have a powerful impact on academic performance in general, and in particular on how students behave and perform in the face of challenge. A core mindset that supports perseverance is called the growth mindset.
(U.S. Department of Education, 2013, p. viii)

✦ *Effortful control:* When we are able to regulate our attention and stay motivated when facing long-term goals.
✦ *Strategies and tactics:* Those of us who are able to persevere do so by using specific strategies to deal with setbacks. The report noted that children "need actionable skills for taking responsibility and initiative, and for being productive under conditions of uncertainty—for example, defining tasks, planning, monitoring, changing course of action, and dealing with specific obstacles" (U.S. Department of Education, 2013, p. viii).

The bottom line is that in order to have a growth mindset home environment, the people who live in the home should work toward developing skills and strategies needed for perseverance and resiliency. Supporting, reinforcing, and modeling these skills is a powerful way to nurture growth mindset thinking in children.

Resiliency is the ability to bounce back from setbacks. It is difficult to build resiliency in our kids if they do not face setbacks very often. If we over-help our children with homework so that they will always be successful, we are not helping them build resiliency. If a child is underchallenged in school, and never has to struggle, then resiliency is slow to develop. Some children who are underchallenged seem to glide through school with effortless success—then, the first time that they must struggle (sometimes not until college), they fall apart. If we catch our children before they fall, then resiliency is not built. Struggle is not a terrible thing. Productive struggle is what contributes to building resiliency. We must allow our children to experience struggle and failure in order to build resiliency, a skill that will help them throughout their life. Perhaps you are a single parent or have gone through a challenging divorce. Maybe you have lost a job through downsizing, or a company move. What strategies have you used to face these challenges? Did some work better than others? Did you take a few minutes to reflect on what responses were helping and what was not? These are the same questions that our children can use when they reflect on challenging situations.

> *Struggle is not a terrible thing. Productive struggle is what contributes to building resiliency.*

WHAT IS GRIT?

No, it is not something to eat for breakfast, nor part of a title of an old John Wayne movie. Grit is the capability to maintain effort toward very long-term goals—kind of like perseverance with a few energy drinks added. Let's think about that for a minute—what is a very long-term goal for a 4-year-old? For some it might be learning to throw or catch a ball, maybe using scissors, or building a block structure. Long-term is relative to the age of the child. As children get older, goals may center on working toward improving an athletic skill, earning income, reaching a level in music, etc. Grit involves "stick-to-it-ive-ness" over time.

Want to find out how "gritty" you are? One resource that you can use is Angela Duckworth's grit scale. A 12-item scale for adults, as well as an 8-item scale for children can be found at this site: https://ange laduckworth.com/grit-scale/.

These scales give adults and children an idea of how "gritty" they are. If you or your child has a low "grit" score, then make a conscious effort to improve your or their ability to stick with a goal after a less-than-successful task, performance, project, or goal. Set a long-term goal to work toward. Always wanted to learn to play the piano? Write a blog or book? Cook every recipe in Julia Child's *Mastering the Art of French Cooking?* (Oh wait, that has been done before! But if you haven't done it, go ahead and try it!) As you work toward a long-term goal, be diligent about your actions. Talk to friends and family members who have shown perseverance and demonstrated grit throughout their lives. Ask them how they stuck with it.

As our children grow older, we want to encourage them to stick with something over a long period of time so that they can practice "grit." It does not have to be an academic area. It might be collecting something, playing an instrument, doing community service, or something completely different.

WHY FAILURE IS IMPORTANT

It is always difficult to see our children fail, especially if much effort was put into accomplishing the task. Think about a time when your child dedicated himself to studying for a test, working on a paper, or practicing a skill and then failed. Failure can be a reward—so to speak—because it is through failure that we can learn the most.

Remember when your child learned to walk? Chances are they wobbled, stumbled, and toppled over many, many times. You knew that this was all part of the process of learning to walk. Sure, you may have put some things in place to support their endeavor—perhaps holding their hands, making sure they had the right shoes, giving them small goals like moving from a sofa to a chair—but you also allowed them to fall. They learned to walk through trying different strategies, practicing, and persevering. It is likely that they faced challenges and obstacles along the way (a toy left in their path, a new pair of [heavy] shoes, a goal that was just a little too far for them), but they demonstrated resilience every time they tumbled and got up again. Your little one demonstrated a growth mindset! There is a terrific picture book, *Walk On! A Guide for Babies of All Ages* by Marla Frazee (Harcourt, 2008), that serves as a great metaphor for learning to do many things for the first time: you will need support, you will need to be careful of things that are wobbly, you may need to get a grip and pull yourself up, and it is important to find your balance, breathe, and look toward where you want to go.

There is a wonderful scene in Disney's *Meet the Robinsons* movie where Lewis creates an invention that combines peanut butter and jelly and it fails. As he buries his face in his hands and apologizes, the adults happily yell, "You've failed! From failure you learn, from success ... not so much" (https://youtu.be/LmW3H-EXYS0). It is a great scene to show your children and an example of how you can use media to demonstrate powerful growth mindset thinking.

When children consciously take the opportunity to learn from all of their errors, they will approach the unsuccessful task in a new way or with more effort. Children who believe that any negative outcome is based on their perceived natural or genetic ability will often not bother to try harder after failure; it is then that we might hear our children say things like, "I am just not good at science," "I will never be able to learn another language," or "It doesn't matter if I do it again, I will have the same results" (Ricci, 2018).

> When children consciously take the opportunity to learn from all of their errors, they will approach the unsuccessful task in a new way or with more effort.

Angel Perez, the dean of admissions at Pitzer College in California, interviews students who apply for admission to his institution and asks this question: "What do you look forward to the most in college?" On one occasion, he heard a response that took him by surprise: "I look forward to the possibility of failure." This potential student continued, "You see, my parents never let me fail, taking a more rigorous course or trying an activity I may not succeed in, they tell me it will ruin my chances at college admission" (Perez, 2012, para. 2). Parents who do all that they can to prevent their children from failing are doing them a disservice—they are keeping them from learning to become resilient.

Learning to embrace failure is a challenge; however, if we all learn about basic brain science (see chapter 4), we can understand why failure is an important part of learning. Children who internalize the understanding of neuroplasticity and the changes that occur in the brain when we learn can deal more constructively with setbacks. They are also sometimes more motivated to work toward mastery and will persist and persevere until they succeed (Ricci, 2018).

Some of our children hold a "bring it on" approach to learning and embrace challenge with enthusiasm. These kids realize that they may not be successful and might even fail a task or two or three or four but want to take the risk and stretch themselves. Other kids feel threatened by challenge, are afraid they will not have success, and will often give up before they put much effort into the task. We need to work toward building a climate at home where mistakes and failure are accepted, and our children learn to reflect and redirect so that they can approach a challenging task in a new way or with more focused effort.

Ever hear of the phrase "helicopter parent?" This term refers to parents who "hover" (much like a helicopter does) over their children in a way that both micro-manages their actions and lessens their chance of experiencing failure. Helicopter parenting does not allow for independence and therefore lessens a child's probability of facing major setbacks and experiencing failure. Same goes with "snowplow parenting" (or lawnmower or bulldozer parenting—what's with the vehicle analogies?), a parenting style that seeks to pave the way for children to have success so they don't experience failure. Think about the college admission scandals that unfolded at various prestigious universities in the United States over the last few years. Some of these parents paved (or paid) the way for their child to be accepted into a college or university through fraudulent SAT scores and/or big donations. Why doesn't this work? Because learning from failure or being disappointed about not getting into a school or on a team, is a vital aspect of not only developing a growth mindset, but also preparing our children for the challenges they will face in the future.

Many of us got caught in an "over-helping" mode during the height of Covid when our children attended school virtually. This led to increased stress for parents and guardians. The Centers for Disease Control surveyed parents and found that approximately 54% of those whose children attended virtual school reported that they suffered from increased emotional distress, 16% said they increased alcohol and drug use, and 21% said they had trouble sleeping (Verlenden et al., 2020). We did not have time to mentally prepare for our kids "doing school" from home because we were juggling ways to safely get groceries, find necessities that were hard to come by, stay healthy, and meet the needs of our families.

If, in the future, we are faced with a similar situation, we need to be aware of over-helping. Yes, we know, it is sometimes hard to watch our children not have success on the first, second, or third try and (let's face it) it is sometimes easier to just jump in and do it for them so that we can get back to work! Instead, we can ask questions that will help them think about the situation or challenge, but we must try to sit on our hands and not jump in to help.

In addition to doing their work for them, some ways that we may be over-helping include:

✦ looking over their shoulder when they are trying to figure something out, which adds stress as well as the likelihood of "opting out" due to frustration or the assumption that the adult will do the task!

✦ making decisions for them, rather than letting them pick out what to wear, how to approach homework, what snack they would like, etc.;

✦ solving conflicts for them when social issues arise in school, sports, or groups of friends;

✦ allowing our own worry or fear to prevent them from participating in age-appropriate activities that may prove to be challenging.

True confession time! One of your authors (OK, it is Mary Cay) has recently fallen into the over-helping trap. Her daughter recently moved into her first apartment in New York City. (Yikes! Time to worry!) She is careful and responsible and has not given Mom reason to think that she can't handle this move. However, Mom found herself giving way too many suggestions: make sure you are in a safe neighborhood, check the building for critters, ensure that you have window and door locks, and on and on. Mom noticed after a while that her daughter's text responses were "ik" (I know) or "I got this," no matter which questions that she asked: "Did you line the cabinets in the kitchen? Clean the bathroom?" Only when her daughter's responses started to get borderline snarky did Mom realize that by making suggestions and asking questions, she was communicating the idea that she didn't think her daughter could handle it. It was Mom's own worry that caused her to morph into that helicopter, snowplow parent. For those of you who have younger children, you may think that by the time your kids get out in the world you will not have to worry so much ... Ha! Just wait and see.

In the book, *How to Raise an Adult: Break Free of the Overparenting Trap and Prepare Your Kid for Success,* author, and former Stanford dean, Julie Lythcott-Haims (2015) explained that when we don't allow our kids opportunities to struggle and fail, we are actually doing them a disservice. She put it this way:

> Depriving our kids of the chance to struggle and to learn to persevere, while we focus instead on prepping them to be the number one at all things and tell them how awesome they are, is a prime example of our best intentions gone awry. Perhaps we didn't realize that "protecting" our kids from falls and failures could hurt them. But it can. We need to redefine success as being a good and kind person, and as making a strong effort whether they ultimately win or lose. We need to help our children gain resilience to cope when things don't go their way.
>
> (Lythcott-Haims, 2015, p. 230)

We all want to relieve the stress of children that we love, but we rarely step back to think about the possible benefits that kids gain from figuring out sticky situations on their own. As mindset researcher David Yeager and his colleagues wrote in a 2022 study:

> 'Stress avoidance' mentality ignores the reality that elevated levels of stress are normal, and in many ways, even a desirable feature of adolescence. Adolescents must acquire a wide and varied array of complicated social and intellectual skills as they transition to adult social roles and prepare for economic independence. This developmental process is inherently stressful, but it is also essential to the task of becoming an adult.
>
> (Yeager et al., 2022)

We need to work toward building a climate at home where mistakes and failure are accepted and our children learn to reflect and redirect so that they can approach a challenging task in a new way or with more focused effort.

"The Gift of Failure: 50 Tips for Teaching Students How to Fail Well" (Chesser, 2013) provided tips for how to teach students how to fail. Parents can easily use this list as well.

A few of the highlights on the list include:

+ teach them to take responsibility;
+ teach them to start over (we would add: teach them how to evaluate *when* they should start over—starting over at early stages of struggle does not build grit and resiliency);
+ foster curiosity;
+ let them cry, whine, and complain (we would add: "sometimes");
+ teach them to care—emphasize humility.

INVENTIONS CREATED BY MISTAKE

Errors and failures can sometimes work out even better than the intended goal—a concept worthy of sharing with your children. A video that will spark some discussion is *10 Accidental Inventions* (ages twelve and up) found at www.youtube.com/watch?v=IqAr HwtvE9Y.

This video highlights how some of the things we eat and use every day were invented by mistake—items such as popsicles, Teflon, Slinkies, and penicillin. Another video that can spark some discussion is 5 *Everyday Things Invented by Accident* (ages 5 and up) found at www.youtube.com/watch?v=w0f0tcqjQP8.

We also love the video, *14 Foods Invented by Complete Accident*—a fun one to watch as a family, www.youtube.com/watch?v=V_2ENsiBzEA.

After watching and discussing the videos, kids can explore other things that were invented thanks to a failure. Other things invented by mistake include:

✦ **foods:** Wheaties, corn flakes, potato chips, chocolate chip cookies, ice cream cones, nachos, tofu, cheese puffs, Coca-Cola, and popsicles;

✦ **toys:** Silly Putty, frisbees, Play-Doh, and the Slinky;

✦ **everyday items:** matches, microwave oven, Velcro, super glue, Teflon, plastic, and Post-it™ notes;

✦ **medical discoveries**: penicillin, pacemakers, and x-rays.

Mistakes That Worked: 40 Familiar Inventions and How They Came to Be by Charlotte Jones (Delacorte Press, 1914) is a great book for kids of all ages. Learning about and discussing one "mistake" a day for 40 days is a wonderful way to infuse dialogue about the potential value of failure into your daily life at home, perhaps in the car or during a meal.

CHANGING HOW OUR KIDS REACT TO FAILURE

When children fail, they may look at this as a sign of weakness and/or incompetence within themselves, which can lead to our children giving up and/or experiencing more failure. They begin to avoid anything that even looks remotely challenging so that they do not have to face failure. On the other hand, if our children view failure or mistakes as a way to get feedback or reflect on areas that need more attention, they possess an underlying belief that they will, with effort, persistence, and support (that they sought themselves) eventually grasp the learning.

Here are several ideas for helping children learn from failure:

+ Help your child become curious about errors or lack of success. Remind your child that failure is important on the way to success. Model this!

+ Show your child the Michael Jordan *Failure* commercial for Nike (available at www.youtube.com/watch?v=45mMioJ5szc and only 30 seconds long). Talk to your child about what the last line of the video means.

+ Provide some puzzles and games that may create a little struggle for your child. Work together and discuss why struggle shows that you are learning, developing good thinking strategies, and that you can build resiliency.

+ Model and encourage resiliency—the ability to bounce back from errors and failures.

+ When watching TV or a movie with your kids, talk about a character who may have not learned from his or her mistakes.

Ask your children how the situation or story would be different if the person had learned from his or her mistakes (and vice-versa).

✦ Be specific when sharing your own growth mindset stories. For example, you might say, "My supervisor gave me some constructive feedback after I made an error at work. I am grateful for that because she gave me some new strategies to try."

The following is a list of people who have faced failure, overcome adversity, learned from setbacks, and demonstrated a growth mindset at some point in their lives:

✦ **Artists:** Stevie Wonder, Demi Lovato, Elvis Presley, Jennifer Lopez, Beethoven, The Beatles, Vincent Van Gogh, Eminem, Fred Astaire, Ed Sheeran

✦ **Businessmen and businesswomen:** Bill Gates, Simon Cowell, Oprah Winfrey, Soichiro Honda, James Dyson, Martha Stewart, R. H. Macy, Colonel Sanders, Mark Cuban, Steve Jobs

✦ **Authors:** Jack London, Louisa May Alcott, Maya Angelou, Agatha Christie, John Grisham

To read more about learning from failure, consider these links:

✦ *Learning From Mistakes: Why We Need to Let Children Fail* (Bright Horizons, 2021, July 15, www.brighthorizons.com/resources/Article/the-importance-of-mistakes-helping-children-learn-from-failure)—this article provides ideas for parents for encouraging risk-taking and helping children learn from their errors.

✦ *How to Help Kids Learn to Fail* (Beth Arky, Childmind.org, reviewed 2023, May 22, https://childmind.org/article/how-to-help-kids-learn-to-fail/)—this article provides strategies for parents to help kids learn to fail by making it a teachable moment.

✦ *How Children Learn from Failure* (enannysource, 2014, January 22, www.enannysource.com/blog/index.php/2014/01/22/how-children-learn-from-failure)—this article, written for both parents and childcare providers, provides a list of strategies to try when a child is facing failure.

Many of us are tempted to overhelp our children with homework assignments, art projects, first attempts at baking, playing chess, etc. We want our children to be successful, don't we? Not only are we trying to develop growth mindset thinking in our children, but we also need to help our children become more independent and autonomous. We must not step in to help them too quickly, and often, we should not step in at all. Sometimes our motivation to help them is because *we* do not want to be embarrassed by our child's performance, particularly if the outcome is very public—a school contest, a big game, or a sticker chart. The next time that temptation arises, take a breath, step back, and give your children the room they need to experiment, struggle, create, problem-solve, persist, and—yes, sometimes even—fail.

REFERENCES

Chesser, L. (2013). *The gift of failure: 50 tips for teaching students how to fail well.* Retrieved April 10, 2023 from www.opencolleges.edu.au/informed/features/the-gift-of-failure-50-tips-for-teaching-students-how-to-fail/

Lythcott-Haims, J. (2015). *How to raise an adult: Break free of the overparenting trap and prepare your kid for success.* New York, NY: Henry Holt.

Olszewski-Kubilius, P. (2013, October). *Talent development as an emerging framework for gifted education.* Presentation given to Baltimore County Public Schools.

Perez, A. B. (2012). Want to get into college? Learn to fail. *Education Week, 31*(19), 23.

Ricci, M. (2018). *Mindsets in the classroom: Building a growth mindset learning community* (updated ed.). Waco, TX: Prufrock Press.

U.S. Department of Education. (2013). *Promoting grit, tenacity and perseverance: Critical factors for success in the 21st century.* Retrieved April 10, 2023 from https://pgbovine.net/OET-Draft-Grit-Report-2-17-13.pdf

Verlenden J. V., Pampati, S., Rasberry, C. N., et al. (2021). Association of Children's Mode of School Instruction with Child and Parent Experiences and Well-Being During the COVID-19 Pandemic—COVID Experiences Survey, United States, October 8–November 13, 2020. *Morbidity and Mortality Weekly Report, 70,* 369–376. DOI: http://dx.doi.org/10.15585/mmwr.mm7011a1external icon

Yeager, D. S., Bryan, C. J., Gross, J. J., Murray, J. S., Krettek Cobb, D., Santos, P. H. S., Gravelding, H., Johnson, M., & Jamieson, J. P. (2022). A synergistic mindsets intervention protects adolescents from stress. *Nature, 607*(7919), 512–520. https://doi.org/10.1038/s41586-022-04907-7

WHAT ABOUT MINDSETS IN SCHOOL?

"I wish that there wasn't so much pressure to get straight 'A's.
I would take harder classes if I could risk getting a B."

—Adam, age 16

Many of us have naturally embraced growth mindset thinking as simply a part of who we are. Long before the advent of the terms *fixed mindset* and *growth mindset,* some parents valued their child's effort and perseverance more than outcome. The conundrum that some of us face is that the message is often not the same in school. Many practices and policies in schools send messages that can reinforce fixed mindset thinking. Some class policies ascribe to a "sink or swim" philosophy which does not recognize failure as a part of the learning process. In addition to these policies and practices, there may be teachers, counselors, and school administrators who do not understand neuroplasticity and that learning is a growth process. On the other hand, many schools have embraced the concept of a growth mindset environment. While this is a welcome development in schools and classrooms, it is important that those educators realize that putting up posters that say, "Have a growth mindset!" is an ineffective and oversimplified way to cultivate a culture of perseverance, effort, and hard work. In this chapter, we'll share some

DOI: 10.4324/9781003405931-7

of the best growth mindset cultures we have seen in schools, and we'll also share some potential pitfalls.

If your children attend schools where the staff and administrators are building a growth mindset environment—awesome! Perhaps you are even reading this book as part of a parent book club for your school. If your children do not attend a school where a growth mindset environment is practiced, you may be wishing they would and looking for ways to bring up the topic with your child's school.

COMPONENTS OF A GROWTH MINDSET SCHOOL

The four most important components that schools should strive for when building a growth mindset learning environment (Ricci, 2020)are:

+ equitable access to advanced learning opportunities;
+ deliberate cultivation of psychosocial skills such as perseverance and resiliency;
+ student understanding of neural networks in the brain;
+ growth mindset feedback and praise.

> If the work that children are asked to do is too easy, there are few opportunities to develop a growth mindset.

These are components that every school should set as goals if it is working toward a growth mindset environment. A safe and secure learning environment must ground these four components. "Safe and secure" doesn't mean just physical security. It means that children and adults must feel safe to try new things, take on challenges, and encounter failure if it is part of the journey to success. Additionally, the learning environment must be full of opportunities for intellectual risk-taking, as well as access to challenging and rigorous instruction and curriculum. If the work that children are asked to do is too easy, there are few opportunities to develop a growth mindset. The first of these components, *equitable access to advanced learning opportunities*, is also very important for parents. As a parent, if you feel that your child does not have access to challenging learning opportunities due to low expectations or fixed mindset thinking from the teacher, this should be discussed. For example, Ciara, your elementary school age daughter, comes home and shares that she is not permitted to do the advanced math work that some of her classmates are doing because she is not identified as "gifted." (Yes, this really happens.) The advanced math would meet her needs as she works hard and demonstrates math skills strong enough to handle the accelerated program. The school, however, has a practice in place for "gifted and talented" identification that looks at strength and above-average performance in all content areas. What should you do? Some questions need to be asked that may bring clarity or will allow the school to reflect on their practices. Start by talking to the teacher. Here are some ideas to get a conversation started:

✦ Ciara shared with me that she would like the challenge of the enrichment math group. Do you think that Ciara could be successful in the enrichment math group? Why or why not?

✦ I have noticed that she picks up mathematical concepts quickly and doesn't quit until she figures out a problem. Do you notice the same?

✦ Since we agree that being in the enrichment group would best fit Ciara's needs, what are the next steps to make that happen?

If the teacher recommends that she needs to wait to be rescreened for "gifted and talented," that means that the process for identification is leaning towards a fixed mindset philosophy. A "gifted" test is just one snapshot of a child—she should not have to be identified as "gifted" to get what she needs instructionally. If strict guidelines and testing windows are in place, then ask if a temporary or trial placement is possible. There is no national standard/process for identification of "gifted." A child could have one foot in one school district and another in the school district next door, and one foot is "gifted" and the other is not. Let the school know that the "gifted" label is unimportant to you, and you are just interested in meeting your child's needs in the regular classroom. Where schools are cultivating a growth mindset environment, a label will never get in the way of an instructional grouping need.

It is also possible that your child is right where he or she should be, and that the teacher does provide opportunities through both ongoing assessment and student observation. The teacher may look for opportunities to provide extra challenge because of your conversation. In some cases, it is possible that a student is not provided with access to higher level learning experiences due to the teacher's perception of the child's intelligence (fixed mindset thinking) or perhaps everyone in the classroom gets the exact same daily lessons, regardless of mastery or need. This is a more challenging situation for a parent, because communicating the concept of malleable intelligence and growth mindset is not a typical conversation in a parent-teacher conference. However, as an example, conversations with the teachers could include some of the following conversation starters:

+ Christopher becomes much more engaged in learning when he feels challenged.
+ I noticed that Christopher tends to do better on tasks that require critical thinking. Have you noticed the same thing?
+ Christopher loves a challenge. Does he seek out challenges in your class?
+ I noticed that he is much more motivated when faced with a challenge.
+ What does Christopher need to do to have access to some higher-level thinking tasks?

If a child is underchallenged, how will important psychosocial skills like persistence and resiliency be developed? Student groupings and grades often lead children to develop fixed mindset views of their intelligence and learning potential.

We would advise starting with the classroom teacher and personalizing your conversation to your own child's performance. Here are some suggestions about what to say during your conversation with your child's teacher:

1. *Always start with a positive.* Tell the teacher something that your child loves about her class. "Bella loves the way you read out loud. It is so animated and engaging. It has really piqued her interest in reading."

2. *Share what brings out the best at home.* Include a relationship between resilience, motivation, effort, or other aspects you want to be addressed. Show how this changes the child's performance. Be as specific as possible. For example, "I have found that Bella really responds well when I praise her persistence when working on a homework assignment."

3. *Share what does not work.* Again, keep your own principles in mind. For example, "I noticed that when I remark on her final product, instead of the process/effort she used to get there, she is not as receptive to suggestions."

4. *Establish the partnership.* Make the teacher part of the plan of action that incorporates your beliefs, as well as his or her practices (and both of your best interests for the child). For example, say, "I would love for us to come up with some common language to use with her so that she will hear a consistent message at home and at school and will put forth her best effort."

Even though these examples do not specifically use the terms *growth* and *fixed mindsets,* they still philosophically address the elements of a growth mindset. You cannot change a person's belief system; you can only present ways that will allow others to reflect on their beliefs and expectations. Even if a teacher does not have a growth mindset belief system, at a minimum the praise language that is used can make a small contribution to a growth mindset culture (Ricci, 2018).

Parents need to gauge the level of information to share based on the openness of the teacher and school administrator. At minimum, parents could stop by the principal's office or send an e-mail to a teacher or administrator with a message such as, "I found this really interesting book/article about mindsets and education that you also might find interesting" (perhaps *Mindsets in the Classroom* by Mary Cay Ricci). Parents can then provide the resources or link to the resource in an e-mail.

However, things do not always go as planned. For example, during a parent-teacher conference, a parent mentioned to a science teacher that their child did not feel like she could be successful in science due in part to a previous negative experience in science. (A previous teacher told the child that she was "just not a science person.") Of course, the hope in sharing that information would be a response that would assure the parent that the teacher would send positive messages her daughter's way, help her daughter anyway that he can, and praise all the effort she puts forth. Well, not so much. His response was … wait for it … "Oh."

Yes, just "Oh."

The parent then tried to engage him in a discussion about growth mindset. It was a one-sided discussion. The parent decided then that she would take matters into her own hands and really bump up her efforts in reminding her daughter about having a growth mindset, persevering, and that her brain was malleable, and she can get smarter! This parent had talked to their daughter many, many times about growth mindset, but now it was completely framed around science. The parent realized a few things during this time, the most important being that children really need to hear and feel the same message at school and at home. Hearing it from a parent is just not enough for some children. Kids need teachers to believe in them as much as their parents do.

Another lesson that we learned is that if you talk to a 12-year-old about the same thing ad nauseam, then you will get "the hand"—as in the "Stop, I have heard this from you a thousand times before and it is not helping" hand gesture. In hindsight, Mom should have arranged another meeting with her child's teacher (with research on mindsets in hand) to make one last attempt to share the research about malleable intelligence and hopefully adjust his messaging to include "effort" praise when responding to her child's performance in science.

Around the time that the first edition of this book was published (2016), schools around the world were rushing to figure out how to use Carol Dweck's mindset research to improve the achievement of students. As is so often the case in education, there is not an easy path from the research that happens in universities to the teachers in the classroom of the school across the street. Educators who are informed by research must make decisions about what its implementation looks like within their own classes with their own students. Sometimes, they simplify the message to the point where the research is misguided. This happened in some places with mindsets.

By now, you know enough about growth mindset to understand how this could happen. It sounds easy enough to promote hard work and effort and to encourage students to "have a growth mindset" rather than giving up on tasks; however, the reality of forming a growth mindset culture is much more complex. A recent study of growth mindset and intellectual risk taking showed that:

> although 77% of teachers claim that they are 'familiar' or 'very familiar' with the concept of growth mindset, many teachers conflate growth mindset with other terms and concepts or have difficulties understanding how to best foster growth mindsets in their students
>
> (Clark & Soutter, 2022)

Carol Dweck herself, in a 2015 opinion column, noted that classrooms tended to emphasize effort but not to include the other facets of her theory (access to challenging work, effective praise, feedback, resiliency, etc.).

Dr. Dan Willingham is a cognitive psychologist at the University of Virginia and author of several bestselling books including *Outsmart Your Brain: Why Learning Is Hard and How You Can Make It Easy* (which we highly recommend for any high school or college student!). "The challenge of changing mindsets should not be underestimated," he said. He went on to point out:

> It's not enough to believe 'all students can learn.' Teachers must act in ways that are consistent with that belief, especially when it comes to the behaviors they encourage and praise…. students' beliefs—and your (educators') beliefs—about intelligence do have an impact, and the question of how to deal with student failure comes up in every classroom. There's good reason for you to put the (growth mindset) research to work.
>
> (Willingham, 2022)

> *The growth mindset teacher will work with the student and guide him or her, help him or her to approach the learning in a new way, and provide a time and space for practice.*

CONSTRUCTIVE FEEDBACK AND REDOS

A recent shift in education has allowed many educators to encourage students to redo assignments and retake assessments. This is especially effective when supports are in place that will help students learn the information in a new way or practice and apply the information. If a teacher truly believes in the importance of errors as a learning device and students are trying to learn from mistakes, then feedback, rather than a grade, should be given on the student's first attempt. The growth mindset teacher will work with the student and guide him or her, help him or her to approach the learning in a new way, and provide a time and space for practice. According to education author Rick Wormeli (2011):

> Many teachers reason that they are building moral fiber and preparing students for the working world by denying them the opportunity to redo assignments and assessments—or if they do allow retakes, by giving only partial credit for redone assessments even when students have demonstrated full mastery of the content. These are the same teachers who set a deadline for submitting work and then give students who do not meet the deadline a zero, thinking that the devastating score will teach them responsibility.
>
> In reality, these practices have the opposite effect: They retard student achievement and maturation. As hope wanes,

resentment builds. Without hope—especially hope that teachers see the moral, competent, and responsible self inside them, waiting to shed its immature shell—students disengage from the school's mission and the adults who care for them. Our education enterprise is lost.

(p. 22–26)

About now you might be thinking: "Well, I thought that you said failure is not a bad thing for kids to experience" (chapter 5). That is still true. Allowing redos allows students to learn from those errors and, most important, learn and master the material that is being taught.

BUT MY CHILD IS A MATH GENIUS!

We tend to have stereotyped ideas about who is good in math and who is not. This mindset about math is fixed. Believing that there are "math people" and "not math people" perpetuates fixed mindset thinking. We both know that this pervasive myth about math—along with the related (and also untrue!) left brain/right brain distinction—is a frustration to great math teachers at all levels.

Right about now, you might be thinking that you don't believe this because math has come easily or quickly for one or more of your kids. That may be true at a young age, but as math becomes more complex, even those children who grasped concepts quickly at an early age will need to put in the time and effort to gain understanding and mastery of multistep and complex concepts. Without the tenacity to approach challenging math concepts, a child could potentially think, "Well, maybe I am not a 'math person' after all." Much of the research around mindsets in the classroom has focused on math. Students who identified their math classrooms as "growth mindset" oriented reported that their teachers talked about how struggle and frustration are natural parts of the learning process and shared accountability for students' success (Hooper et.al., 2016).

IT SHOULDN'T ALWAYS WORK

One of the school district superintendents we have been fortunate to know had a tradition of meeting with a group of graduating students from every high school in their district prior to the end of the school year to gain informal feedback and insights about their experiences. At one of these listening sessions, a most surprising piece of advice for the superintendent came from two students who were working at a prestigious cancer research laboratory as part of their final semester of high school. "Make sure some of the science experiments don't work," the students said.

Every science experiment we did in school "worked." They never failed. We've discovered by being interns that in the real world, the experiments might fail for years and years before they "work." Everyone in science classes should have the experience of something failing and having to redo it or uncover why it didn't work.

This recognition of the realities of high-level scientific research can also be applied to many trades, industries, and fields of study. As educators, it is important that we develop cultures of growth that help students to see failure as part of a cycle that must be overcome to reach success.

AWARDS ASSEMBLIES

Awards programs and assemblies elicit accolades for those children who reach a specific level of performance, but rarely consider that some winners put forth little effort to reach the mark and others put forth tremendous effort and missed it by a thread. An educator in Colorado explained that in her school they hold Honor Roll assemblies quarterly and the same kids are always sitting in the back two rows—those who are never recognized. What is the point of an Honor Roll assembly? If the response is to recognize good grades, we would argue that the "reward" was the grade. Also important to note is that some of the 'A's were given without a whole lot of effort from the students (these students were underchallenged). If the response is to motivate others, then take note: Are the same students going unrecognized every time? Does an Honor Roll assembly really motivate others? An event such as this should shift its purpose to celebrate growth and hard work rather than grades.

PARENT ASSOCIATIONS

Local school-parent associations can also get involved in the mindset message. In some schools, a representative from the parent association is invited to participate in a few of the school planning meetings. These meetings may be an ideal time to bring up the importance of a growth mindset school setting. Offer to form a mindset committee at the school and invite other parents and teachers to be part of the committee. When the committee is formed, agenda items could include some of the following things:

- events for educating the parent community about mindsets;
- book club ideas;
- game nights—a great opportunity for adults and children to practice perseverance and resiliency together; and
- a mindset resource page as part of the school portal or website.

A sample mindset parent webpage can be found in *Ready-to-Use Resources for Mindsets in the Classroom* (Ricci, 2020) as well as sample newsletter blurbs. As a parent group, you may want to send growth mindset goals for parents every few weeks, perhaps something like Figure 6.1, Creating a Growth Mindset Environment at Home, which contains many of the ideas that have been already discussed in this

IDEAS FOR CREATING A GROWTH MINDSET ENVIRONMENT AT HOME

Ideas for Creating a Growth Mindset Environment at Home Part 1:
Parents Work Toward a Growth Mindset for Themselves

- We can't expect our children to have a growth mindset if we don't have one ourselves. Recognize fixed mindset thinking in yourself and talk yourself into a growth mindset. This can also be done out loud so that your child can hear how you are changing your mindset. For example, you might catch yourself saying, "I can't figure out how to fill out this document." Then quickly rephrase it to add, "I think I need to check on the website or call the bank so I can ask some questions. Then I am sure I will be able to fill it out accurately."

- Be aware of your own fixed mindset statements such as "I am a terrible cook," "I was never good at math either," or "I wish I could play the piano like you do." (You can, with practice and perseverance!)

- Be aware of blaming genetics for anything—both positive and negative.

- Be careful about comparing your kids to their siblings or other kids.

- We want our children to enjoy the process of learning—not just be successful. Model this concept at home. For example, after a less than desirable outcome trying to bake something challenging, you might say "I really learned a lot making those cookies" rather than "Ugghh, what a waste of time. That was an epic fail. I will never try that recipe again."

FIGURE 6.1 CREATING A GROWTH MINDSET ENVIRONMENT AT HOME

Source: Ricci (2020, pp. 67–70). Reprinted

Ideas for Creating a Growth Mindset Environment at Home Part 2:
Using Growth Mindset Praise and Feedback

- Praise what your child does, not who he or she is. Instead of saying, "You are so smart/clever/brilliant," say "I can see you really worked hard/put forth effort/tried hard." Praise perseverance and resiliency when you see your child struggle or face challenge. Avoid praising grades. Focus on praising work ethic and effort—not achievement.

- Adopt the word "yet" into your vocabulary. If your child proclaims that he doesn't understand something, can't dribble a basketball, or can't play a song on his guitar, remind him that he can't "yet" but with hard work he will have success.

- Avoid comparing your child's success with that of siblings or friends—achievement is not a competition. There is enough success for everyone.

Ideas for Creating a Growth Mindset Environment at Home Part 3:
Redirecting Fixed Mindset Thinking

- Redirect your child's fixed mindset statements. If you hear your child say "I am no good in math" or "I just can't understand Shakespeare," point out the fixed mindset thinking and direct her to a growth mindset place. Remind her that she may not understand yet, but will by asking questions, finding new strategies, setting small goals, and working hard. Two examples of how to redirect such statements are included below.

If Your Child Says	Then You Might Say
"I am no good in math."	"You may not understand this yet, so let's practice some more."
"I don't need to study; I always do well on math assessments."	"Studying can help prime the brain for further growth. Maybe you should let your teacher know that these assessments don't require much practice for you and that you are willing to take on more challenge."

FIGURE 6.1 CONTINUED

Ideas for Creating a Growth Mindset Environment at Home Part 4:
Struggle

- Help your child become curious about errors or lack of success. Remind your child that failure is important on the way to success. Model this!

- Show your child the Michael Jordan Failure commercial (available at https://www.youtube.com/watch?v=45mMioJ5szc and only 30 seconds long). Talk to your child about what the last line of the video means.

- Provide some puzzles and games that may create a little struggle for your child. Work together and discuss why struggle shows that you are learning and that you can build resiliency.

- Model and encourage resiliency—the ability to bounce back from errors and failures.

Ideas for Creating a Growth Mindset Environment at Home Part 5:
Flexibility and Optimism

- Model flexibility. Communicate that change is an important part of living life. Model this by taking a flexible mentality when things don't go as planned. Don't let frustrating situations get the best of you—make your children aware of your ability to adapt due to a change in plans. Praise your children for their flexibility and adaptability when plans change or success is not met.

- Model optimism. Adopt a "glass half full" mentality in your home. A person with "hope" believes there can be a positive side to most situations.

- Play a game with your kids: For every time something happens that is perceived as "bad," try to find the good in every situation. This game can get a little silly but it gets a message of positivity across. For example, when a glass is accidentally broken, a possible response might be, "Now we have more room on our shelf!"

FIGURE 6.1 CONTINUED

Ideas for Creating a Growth Mindset Environment at Home Part 6:
Learning and the Brain

- Talk about neural networking. Ask your child what he or she has learned in school about the brain.

- Whenever you hear your child say "I give up" or "I just don't get this," remind your child to visualize neurons connecting every time he learns something new. Encourage your child to work hard and practice new skills and concepts so that he can develop strong neural connections in his brain.

- Share with your child some things that you have not yet mastered and your plan for practicing and building stronger connections in your brain.

Ideas for Creating a Growth Mindset Environment at Home Part 7:
Developing Important Psychosocial Skills

- A child's innate ability contributes to only about 25% of achievement. The other 75% are psychosocial skills that must be deliberately developed.

  The important skills we can help our children develop include:
  - » perseverance,
  - » self-confidence,
  - » resiliency,
  - » coping skills for disappointment and failure, and
  - » the ability to handle constructive feedback.

- Choose books to read with younger students that highlight characters that demonstrate these skills. Discuss these with your child.

- When watching TV or a movie with your kids, talk about a character's strength or lack of perseverance or resiliency. Ask your children how

FIGURE 6.1 CONTINUED

the situation or story would be different if the person did or did not have this skill.

- Name the psychosocial skills words and use phrases that represent these around the house. For example, you might say, "My supervisor gave me some constructive feedback about how I can do my job better. I am grateful for that because she gave me some new things to try" or "I was watching you (climb that tree, play that video game, figure out the new cell phone, etc.) today. You really showed determination and perseverance!"

FIGURE 6.1 CONTINUED

book. This resource, however, has been broken down into seven sections so that you can set growth mindset goals for yourself or share it with a parent group. Parent associations might support mindsets in the school by providing funding for plush neurons, books, or reasoning games. Nonverbal reasoning games are a wonderful vehicle for developing a growth mindset. In fact, we recommend these for families as well—many are small and fit into a glove compartment in your car. When your kids are waiting for an appointment or you need them to stay occupied while you are meeting with someone, have a few in your bag. When games require reasoning and problem solving, they can contribute to a mindset shift, particularly those games that increasingly get more difficult. As the levels become more challenging, kids develop their perseverance as well as reasoning processes. A study described in *Mindsets in the Classroom* (Ricci, 2018) suggested that individual reasoning games in partnership with growth mindset learning increased motivation for children.

Games we like include:

✦ Chocolate Fix, Brick Logic, Rush Hour, and Rush Hour Jr. (Thinkfun; www.thinkfun.com):

✦ Little Red Riding Hood, Safari Park Jr., Snow White Deluxe, Tangoes, and Three Little Piggies (SmartGames; www. smarttoysandgames.com):

✦ Logic! CASE Starter Puzzle Set (HABA; www.habausa.com):

✦ Little Thinker's Block Logic (Fat Brain Toys; www.fatbraintoys):

✦ Thinkfun also offers free downloadable games and brainteasers (www.thinkfun.com/parents/downloadable-games-brain teasers/):

✦ There are also some great free online logical reasoning games at Number Dyslexia (www.numberdyslexia.com/online-logical-reasoning-games/):

CHILDREN WITH SPECIAL NEEDS

You might be the parent of a child with special needs and wonder if growth and fixed mindset applies to you. It does! Perhaps the best way to communicate the importance of a growth mindset in a child who has unique physical, emotional, or learning challenges is to learn from a very special young man's story.

Troy Baisey came into this world prematurely with cerebral palsy and a learning disability. While being treated for a health issue as a young boy, he was given medication that was ultimately responsible for a serious hearing loss. Challenges during his early childhood included walking, talking, speaking, hearing, and learning to sign. Troy's school experiences included many adjustments and modifications as a special education student with a full-time assistant. By the time Troy was 22 years old, he was taking a few classes at his local community college, working, and volunteering in his community. Because of his own hearing loss, Troy had an interest in working with the deaf and hard of hearing and pursued a certificate in American Sign Language. He serves as an inspirational role model for others who have challenges because his success is the result of hard work, persistence, strong family support, and a growth mindset.

Troy's growth and independence came from the fact that he and his family set incremental goals along the way. We interviewed Troy and his mother, Michele Baisey, to learn more about the ways that Troy overcomes his challenges.

We asked Troy what advice he might give other children with disabilities. He said, "Keep trying your best, learn to advocate for yourself, ask for support when you need it, and do not give up." Troy spoke to the Board of Education in his school district as he completed his public-school education. He shared the following with them:

> I accept my special needs and do the best I can do. I stay positive and believe in myself even when life can be difficult and frustrating. I never gave up on myself and fought through the rough times and am proud of where I am in my life today.

"Keep trying your best, learn to advocate for yourself, ask for support when you need it, and do not give up."—Troy Baisey

Troy's mom, Michele, shared that as she raised Troy it was important to have a support system surrounding her, and she learned to balance and recognize what his immediate needs were while always keeping in mind long-term goals. Michele learned to think ahead and knew that with effort and perseverance Troy would reach his goals. Michele also recognized that learning might have to be approached differently for Troy. Both Troy and Michele view struggle not as a roadblock, but as a learning opportunity. When Troy began taking classes at the local community college, Michele supported Troy in learning to use public transportation so that he could become more independent. Michele views new learning such as this not as an obstacle but just a hurdle to jump over. Troy has also learned to advocate for himself by letting people know when he does and does not need help. He explained that he will ask people to repeat, rephrase, or explain things in a different way so that he can understand.

Because Troy and his mom both have a growth mindset, Troy has demonstrated resiliency throughout his life. What lessons can be learned about parenting children with special needs from Troy's story?

+ Set goals with your child—both short-term and long-term ones.
+ Deliberately cultivate skills such as perseverance, resiliency, and learning from struggle and failure. Make sure your child knows how valuable these skills are.
+ Give your child the tools to advocate for him- or herself.
+ Ensure that the supports provided are appropriate—too much support can be just as detrimental as not enough.
+ Keep a positive, optimistic attitude.
+ Ask for help when you need it! That goes for the parent as well as the child—find the resources available to you and learn all you can about how to utilize them.

COLLEGE

High school graduation is over, bags are packed for college, and your child is ready to begin another part of his or her life journey. Think that your growth mindset reminders are over? Think again. When our children begin college, whether they go away or take courses locally, they have some new skills to learn outside of the classroom: time management, self-advocacy, and learning personal responsibility, to name a few. When the first essay or research paper is due, you may get a text or call asking if you could read it over or give it a final edit. The tricky part is letting your children know that you are there to support them and, at the same time, letting them learn from potential mistakes.

Some college students become less afraid of taking intellectual risks and making mistakes. A college freshman explained that in high school she was always worried about her grade point average (GPA) because the constant messaging (nagging, perhaps) she received in high school was about keeping her grades up so that she could get into college. Once in college, it became less about the grades and more about the actual learning because she no longer had the college admittance worry in the front of her mind. However, this is not always the case. One college student, Monique, really wanted to participate in a semester abroad program that her university offered, but after consulting with some students who had studied overseas previously, she learned that the grading scale was more rigorous. She decided not to have the experience because she was not willing to compromise her GPA. This kind of fixed mindset thinking prevented Monique from an enriching and memorable learning experience. She was too focused on the potential grade and not focused enough on the experience of studying abroad.

> *Too often, children leave for college with the feeling that coursework in their area of interest or passion is supposed to be easy for them, only to find that the course of study they dreamed of is not as easy as they anticipated. In a fixed mindset, having to work harder than classmates or receiving a poor grade in a course that a student "was supposed to be good at" is viewed as a sign that the content is beyond the student's ability.*

It is also important for college students to remember that having to work hard and facing challenging assignments and tasks is part of the learning experience and not a sign of being incapable or in the wrong major. Too often, children leave for college with the feeling that coursework in their area of interest or passion is supposed to be easy for them, only to find that the course of study they dreamed of is not as easy as they anticipated. In a fixed mindset, having to work harder than classmates or receiving a poor grade in a course that a student "was supposed to be good at" is viewed as a sign that the content is beyond the student's ability. This kind of fixed mindset perspective can prompt a college student to prematurely change his or her course of study. It is helpful to encourage college-aged children to spend time talking to their faculty advisors and other academic or accommodation advisors about courses and their expectations. Campus tutoring and resource centers or study groups offer opportunities for students to ask for additional support that they may need and to connect with others who are also working hard.

For our highest achieving students—those few who breezed through elementary, middle, and high school with little or no effort—college is sometimes the first time these students face struggle. Academic resiliency cannot be built if a student has never faced academic struggle. If your child never struggled while in school, perhaps it is because he was underchallenged. We have heard from several parents whose children demonstrated high achievement but never really had to work too hard—that is, until college.

Some colleges have recognized the stress and exhaustion that students are under when they are afraid that they are the only students who think their coursework is challenging. These institutions developed coaching resources and advised faculty that sharing their own challenges might be very helpful as students adjust to the demands of higher education. Recognizing that struggle is often a part of the college experience serves to ensure that students don't give up and change majors at the first sign of a challenge.

One mom described the tearful phone call she received when her daughter received her first B. After consoling her daughter, this mom used the opportunity to reflect on the messaging that she and her husband had communicated to her daughter from a very young age: "We expect you to be an A student." In fact, when the girl's father was asked how his daughter was doing in college, his response was, "We will find out when we see her first semester grades." Ugh! Overemphasis of grades perpetuates fixed mindset thinking and ultimately develops risk-averse adults.

If you recognize yourself in this scenario, it is not too late to adjust feedback to your college-age child. Just remember to focus on the process and strategies that your child is putting in place in college such as time management, use of the library, study groups, self-advocacy, seeking extra help, and the effort that is being put forth. The grades should never be the conversation starter. What message does that send to your young adult? Perhaps messages like these: "Wow, all Dad seems to care about is my grades," or "I wish Mom would ask about how I am adjusting at school rather than my grades all of the time." One young man was involved in a discussion about his first semester of college, and he shared the following:

> It is important to Mom and Dad that I make Dean's list so they can tell all their friends and put it in the local newspaper. It is all about appearances with them. They want people to think they have the perfect child. This stresses me out! I wish they would just let me make some mistakes and learn from them along the way.

A growth mindset perspective will help college students become resilient and ready to face the challenges of graduate school or entering the workforce after graduation.

From preschool through kindergarten, parents strive to raise happy, healthy kids. Growth mindset kids tend to be more optimistic about life in general and don't fall apart easily when things get tough. Sometimes school can undermine your growth mindset goals due to fixed mindset student feedback and fixed mindset policies and practices. We can't overly focus on things that are out of our control like a fixed mindset coach or teacher. Focus on what you can do within your home and family to raise growth-minded individuals so that when they face fixed mindset thinking along the way, they will have the resiliency to meet it head on.

REFERENCES

Clark, S., & Soutter, M. (2022). Growth mindset and intellectual risk taking. *Kappan, 104*(1), 50–55.

Dweck, C. (2015, September 23). Carol Dweck revisits the growth mindset. *Education Week.* Retrieved April 10, 2023 from www.edweek.org/ew/artic les/2015/09/23/carol-dweck-revisits-the-growth-mindset.html

Hooper S. Y., Yeager D. S., Wright C., Haimovitz K., Murphy M. (2016). *Creating a classroom incremental theory matters. But it's not as straightforward as you might think.* Poster presented at the biennial meeting of the Society for Research on Adolescence, Baltimore, MD.

Ricci, M. (2018). *Mindsets in the classroom: Building a growth mindset learning community* (updated ed.). Waco, TX: Prufrock Press.

Ricci, M. (2020). *Ready-to-use resources for mindsets in the classroom: Everything educators need for school success.* Waco, TX: Prufrock Press.

Willingham, D. (2022). Does Developing a Growth Mindset Help Students Learn? *American Educator, Winter 2022–23.*

Wormeli, R. (2011). Redos and retakes done right. *Educational Leadership, 69*(3), 22–26.

CHAPTER 7

HOW CAN I DEVELOP A GROWTH MINDSET FOR MY CHILD IN SPORTS AND THE ARTS?

"Winning is fun, but losing is okay as long as we learned something."

—Priyanka, age 12

For many families, Saturday mornings are not spent in front of the television watching cartoons, but instead are spent on the field or in the dance studio. Children develop critical skills and lifelong enjoyment through their participation in sports and the arts. It is important to consider how a growth mindset orientation can be applied to the valuable activities children pursue outside of the academic arena.

Parents play a pivotal role in nurturing and cultivating growth mindset thinking for their kids in these endeavors. Although much of the time parents are spectators and supporters, parents are often called on to coach their own child and others. Whether as a casual observer, an ardent cheerleader, or a seasoned coach, the role of the parent in developing a growth mindset through sports and the arts is significant.

DOI: 10.4324/9781003405931-8

TALENT, DELIBERATE PRACTICE, OR BOTH?

You have probably heard about the nature versus nurture debate. How much of who you are is the result of heredity, and how much is the result of your environment and your upbringing? It is easy to enter such a debate when considering how much success in sports or the arts is due to innate talent and how much is due to hard work and practice. Based on what we now know about how the brain learns and makes new neural connections (see chapter 4), it is clear that learning and growth contribute mightily to exceptional performance. In a 1992 study in England, researchers set off to look for innate musical talent. By studying the backgrounds of 257 music students, they established that the student musicians at the highest echelons of performance had only one significant musical ability that separated them from the others. Those students had been able to hear a tune and repeat it at a young age. Was this a sign of innate talent? It is possible, but the researchers also determined that those children had been sung to by their parents from a very young age, and that this early exposure to a variety of tunes was most likely responsible for their ability to hear and repeat the musical cadence. Most significantly, the study did reveal that there *was* one factor that separated the preeminent musicians from the others. What was that one factor? Practice. The students who spent the most sustained and focused time in practice rose to the top levels of their musical fields (Aiello & Sloboda, 1994).

Let's examine a few examples of talent in the arts and sports and how mindsets can play a role in these children's lives:

Six-year-old Sam can often be found curled up on the family sofa with a sketchpad and pencil, drawing fanciful characters and detailed scenes from a world born of his imagination. His parents noticed his affinity for art at an early age, when he began attempting to copy comic strips from the newspaper onto scribble pads with crayons and was captivated by a local television program aimed at teaching adults to draw and paint.

Sam's parents were concerned that while it was clear that he enjoyed art, they doubted he had any innate artistic ability because they knew of no family members who had been artists or who had shared his interest.

Sam's neighbor, 12-year-old Damian, has a passion, too, but his is basketball. Damian started watching college hoops on television with his mom when he was a toddler and gradually gained more and more interest. He quickly graduated from a pee-wee basketball hoop in the driveway to a regulation height one in the neighborhood and enjoys playing with high school kids after school and on weekends. He plays in the local recreation league and tells his mom he can't wait to play at the high school he'll attend, which boasts a highly competitive program. Damian has his sights on playing Division I basketball in college. It is a lofty goal, and one that worries Damian's mother. She was involved in drama and debate in high school and college and the sports arena is one that she enjoys as a spectator, but not as an athlete. When he had the pee-wee hoop in the driveway, his mom spent time playing with him, but Damian's mother can't really play basketball with him anymore. Even a game of "HORSE" frustrates both because Damian clearly needs better competition. Like Sam's parents, Damian's mom is concerned that Damian may be held back by heredity and her ever-growing lack of capacity to model and coach him.

There is good news for these parents and others. The recipe for helping a child to be successful in the arts, sports, or academics does not rely on any innate talent on the part of the parent. In fact, noted Australian musician Mimia Margiotta (2011) summed it up well when she said, "Children who are successful with instrumental learning do not necessarily have parents who have musical abilities; in fact, most have parents who simply offer support and encouragement rather than provide expertise and technical knowledge" (p. 17). Joey Chua of the University of Helsinki undertook a 2-year study of 16- to 22-year-olds who were enrolled in national dance institutions, the Finnish National

Opera Ballet School and the Singapore Dance Theatre. The study aimed to determine what types of support during their formative years were most significant in helping these young people reach their high levels of performance. Through a series of wide-ranging interviews with the dancers, their parents, and teachers, Chua (2015) found several key takeaways for parents. Several of the dancers advised that the focus should be "on a lot of hard work and practice" and "determination" rather than relying on innate abilities (p. 184). One parent said, "You can't just escape with no practice but with lots of talent" (p. 184). Dancers stressed the importance of "constant corrections" and "good criticism and good feedback to improve their technique," but found this from their teachers rather than their parents (p. 186). Chua, addressing what is most important in development of dancers, wrote, "Adults should hold a growth mindset ... to impress upon students that sustained effort, in addition to malleable dance abilities, is crucial in dance development" (p. 188).

> The recipe for helping a child to be successful in the arts, sports, or academics does not rely on any innate talent on the part of the parent.

Sometimes our efforts to support and praise our children as they participate in the arts and athletics actually undermine their growth. Parents who believe that their children are the star of the team, the "natural" talent, or a prodigy often communicate this to friends, relatives, and coaches. Children hear this characterization and internalize the expectation that it carries. This is fixed mindset thinking, even though it can be well-intentioned. A child's learning progress is often affected by parents' preconceived ideas about his or her capabilities and these fixed ideas can "impinge on the child's learning progress and leave the child feeling unable to cope and achieve" (Margiotta, 2011, p. 17). When trying to be supportive with comments like "You are the best player I've ever seen!", parents unwittingly create stress and anxiety.

In an article for *The New Yorker,* music critic Alex Ross profiled the career of famed composer Wolfgang Amadeus Mozart. Referencing the bestselling line of Baby Einstein products made popular over the last 15 years, Ross (2006) wrote, "Ambitious parents who are currently playing the 'Baby Mozart' video for their toddlers may be disappointed to learn that Mozart became Mozart by working furiously hard" (para. 15). Although the creators of Baby Einstein videos and toys aim to spark a child's curiosity about the arts, it is evident from the popularity of the products that many parents believe that the toys and programs can cultivate talent. Although engaging a child's interest in the arts is an excellent strategy, Ross aimed to point out that it is not innate talent that makes one successful—it is hard work and practice, two hallmarks of a growth mindset.

> When trying to be supportive with comments like "You are the best player I've ever seen!", parents unwittingly create stress and anxiety.

Swedish psychologist Anders Ericsson, a researcher on expertise, undertook a long-term study of violinists in the early 1990s. Ericsson and his colleagues found that the characteristics that had often been attributed to innate ability were instead the result of deliberate, sustained practice over a minimum of at least 10 years. The elements of deliberate practice, as evidenced by Ericsson and his colleagues, are applicable to sports as well as the arts (Colvin, 2008). These elements include practice that is:

+ designed specifically to improve performance, often with the help of a teacher or coach;
+ repeated a lot;
+ highly demanding, mentally or physically; and
+ supported with specific, directive feedback.

For deliberate practice to lead to the highest levels of performance, it is important for those engaged in the practice to stretch themselves out of their comfort zones. Think back to our discussion of the brain in chapter 4. New neural connections grow when the brain is challenged beyond its comfort zone. Similarly, Noel Tichy, a successful businessman and professor at the University of Michigan, developed a visual representation of three "zones of performance," as referenced in Geoffrey Colvin's (2008) book, *Talent Is Overrated: What Really Separates World-Class Performers From Everybody Else.* These zones, shown in Figure 7.1, can help to illustrate the challenge of staying in the learning zone as a child gains comfort and proficiency with a skill.

It is only by choosing activities in the learning zone that one can make progress. The challenge for parents, teachers, and coaches is to accurately identify where the learning zone is and to keep the child in the learning zone as he or she becomes more skilled (Colvin, 2008). At the same time, adults need to ask themselves:

+ Is the amount of practice impacting other areas of the child's life?
+ Is the level of challenge often motivating? Or is the challenge only frustrating?
+ Do the adults overseeing the practice provide feedback that allows the child to grow?

All this information about practice suggests a quote that has been repeated over and over in the golf world. After watching famous golfer Gary Player hit a fantastic shot, a spectator said, "Wow, I've never seen anyone so lucky in my life!" to which Player replied, "Well, the harder I practice, the luckier I get." Although Player claims to be the originator of the quote, many golfers, including Lee Trevino and Arnold Palmer have spoken the same words on occasion (Yocom, 2010).

PRACTICE

For some children, practice is not a chore, but a sanctuary. In *The Art of Practicing: A Guide to Making Music From the Heart,* Madeline Bruser (1999) pointed out that although the word *practice* conjures up images and feelings of hours of skill drills for some, for others practice can be a sanctuary of "welcome relief from other pursuits and an activity

FIGURE 7.1 ZONES OF PERFORMANCE

Source: Noel Tichy developed a visual representation of three "zones of performance," as referenced in Geoffrey Colvin's (2008) book, *Talent Is Overrated: What Really Separates World-Class Performers From Everybody Else*

in which they feel free to express themselves" (p. 1). Helping to frame practice in this sort of light may help to reduce the need for nagging and cajoling a child to head to the piano or to the dance studio.

Children often have unrealistic expectations of how much they will need to practice a skill, instrument, or technique before they become proficient. When fourth grader Ashante decided that she wanted to play the clarinet in the school band, she pictured herself in band class engaging with the teacher, on the stage performing in concerts, and spending her evenings playing tunes for her family. On the other hand, Ashante's parents, realizing her involvement in scouts, soccer, and church, had concerns about when she would find time to practice. In her 10-year-old mind, Ashante envisioned herself quickly mastering the clarinet and moving to the first chair in the school band. You can imagine how quickly this scenario unraveled when Ashante realized that she had severely underestimated the amount of practice it would take to simply make the clarinet sound like "music" and not like a barking seal. She wanted to quit the band almost as quickly as she started.

This scenario is not unusual, and it can be very frustrating for parents who watch a child bounce from one activity to another, often incurring significant expense and angst along the way. In a 2002 study in the journal *Music Education Research*, Gary E. McPherson and Jane W. Davidson pointed out what likely halted Ashante's musical endeavors:

> Children who ceased learning typically had unrealistically high expectations about how much practice they would undertake even before commencing lessons. After they started, and the reality of learning set in, they also consistently undertook less practice than their peers who chose to continue.
> (McPherson and Davidson, 2002, p. 152)

They also said that while a wide range of factors influence the skills required to learn a musical instrument, "sustained musical involvement will only occur when certain conditions are met. One of the most important is the parent or guardian, who is a critical motivator of practice" (McPherson & Davidson, 2002, p. 142).

Practice, whether it be on the piano, in the pool, or on the football field, is not always easy and it is not always fun. Most of the time it is not glamorous, either. One of your authors (Meg) is learning a new art form, knitting. (It is supposed to relax your mind and be a sort of meditative practice, but that part hasn't happened YET!) Learning to knit requires a great deal of practice, first of each stitch and then of a variety of techniques that are required for making different projects. For instance, it might take several tries to make a hat that doesn't have mysterious-looking holes in it. It requires perseverance, commitment, and time. It also requires the support and feedback of a teacher or coach. In Meg's case, she works with her knitting teacher, Emily, once a week and sends pictures of knitting projects in-process to get feedback and pointers. Practice allows the brain time to make solid neural connections and grow new ones with increasing levels of challenge. As the knitting skills become more advanced, Meg is recognizing that the more she practices, the more easily she can take on the next challenging project. She is building strong neural connections as she knits, and those connections enable her to complete some simple stitches almost automatically while she concentrates on newer skills that are completely new neural connections. As a parent, you can help your child get the most out of this need for practice by framing it in the context of growing and improving. Figure 7.2 provides suggestions for helping you do this.

> *Practice allows the brain time to make solid neural connections and grow new ones with increasing levels of challenge.*

In Mindset: The New Psychology of Success, Carol Dweck (2006) issued a valuable reminder to parents: "Parents often set goals their children can work toward. Remember that having innate talent is not a goal. Expanding skills and knowledge is. Pay careful attention to the goals you set for your children" (pp. 211–212).

CHEERING FROM THE SIDELINES

We have all experienced the discomfort of being on the sidelines at a sporting event and hearing a parent yell at the children, the referees, and the coaches. In her book *How to Raise an Adult,* former Stanford dean Julie Lythcott-Haims (2015) summed it up well when she said, "Kids' sports are one arena in which parents often fail so badly as role models that our behavior requires apology" (p. 33). It can be hard to maintain a growth mindset when you watch your child making mistakes, not giving 100%, or being corrected by a coach or an official. We all sometimes get wrapped up in the excitement of the event and forget that the messages we send are powerful and can influence whether our children are developing a growth mindset or a fixed mindset.

In a growth mindset, cheering from the sidelines of a sporting event or performance includes acknowledging the child's efforts ("Good

FIGURE 7.2 SUGGESTIONS FOR EFFECTIVE PRACTICE

work!"), encouraging risk taking ("Go for it!") and praising growth ("That's it!"). These messages from parents reinforce the growth mindset while allowing the child to fully participate in the activity taking place. In some cases, standing on the sidelines means hearing a parent coach a child through every motion of the dance or every play of the game. If children are constantly relying on direction from the sidelines, they become a listener and not a creator of the action. Rather than learning to solve their own problems on the stage or the field, they are relieved of that responsibility and instead rely on the parent or adult to direct their next action. This micromanagement of the child creates a lack of self-sufficiency and sends a fixed mindset message.

John O'Sullivan, founder and CEO of Changing the Game Project, said, "Coaches and parents who keep a running commentary on the sideline, second-guessing every decision and action players take, and yelling at players for trying their best and failing, create a culture of fear that drives players from the game" (O'Sullivan, 2015, para. 19). No one wants to see young people quit sports, but recent research shows that 70% of children drop out of organized sports by the age of 13. The reason? It isn't fun. Exercise science professor Amanda Visik from George Washington University surveyed 150 children about what they find fun about sports. Eighty-one factors emerged. Winning was number 48. High on the list: positive team dynamics, trying hard, positive coaching, and learning (Rosenwald, 2015). Figure 7.3 shares a list of ideas for the things you *should* be saying while standing on the sidelines.

MAKING THE TEAM: A GROWTH MINDSET APPROACH

Few moments are more stressful for families than sports tryouts, particularly at the high school or club sports levels. We had the good fortune to follow two rising high school freshman boys as they prepared to try out for their respective soccer teams at two different schools.

Although both boys had successful freshman soccer seasons, one had an experience that is much more growth mindset oriented than the other.

We met Jeff Colsh, varsity soccer coach at Middletown High School in Maryland, after the mother of one of his freshman players noticed something unusual in her son's summer preparation for soccer tryouts and pointed it out to us as an example of growth mindset. Her son, Dominic, had attended an informational meeting about playing high school soccer and came home with a skills card that recorded his level of play in several key areas. Coach Colsh and his assistant coach, Anthony Welch, set up a pre-skills night in May for any player interested in trying out for soccer in August. They set up a series of stations and modeled what the players were supposed to do at each station. Then they rotated the potential players through the stations and recorded the results. No targets for performance were given, but at the end of the event, Colsh and Welch suggested that players should go home and compete against themselves to attempt to improve upon the drill scores by the August tryouts. Each player was given a small card on which the coaches had recorded the station results (see Figure 7.4 for an example of Colsh's feedback sheet). At regular intervals throughout the summer, Dominic recreated the skills stations in his backyard and set about improving his performance. He wanted to grow and improve by the tryouts, and he did.

Jacob was also a rising ninth grader who wanted to play soccer, far from Middletown. He also attended a May information night, but it wasn't a skills clinic. It was a presentation about the requirements of sports participation, the medical forms, and the schedule. Although the information was valuable, there was only one mention of goals or performance to be prepared for the August tryouts: "If you want to make the Junior Varsity team, you must run a 7-minute mile. To make varsity, you must run a 6-minute mile. Follow the conditioning plan over the summer."

When Jacob got in the car after the soccer meeting, he was asked what he was going to do to get ready for the August tryouts. "I don't need to do anything," he replied. "I can already run a 6-minute mile." This was true. By setting a fixed mark for performance, Jacob's coach had communicated an expectation that Jacob could already fulfill. Although the coach likely thought that the timed mile targets would be a wake-up

CHEERING ON THE SIDELINES

We often hear parents saying things like, "Make the shot!" and "You're the best!" from the sidelines of sporting events. Although well-intentioned, these comments can reinforce a fixed mindset. Here is a list of growth-mindset language that an adult could use to support a child during a sporting event or competition.

+ I love how hard you are working! Keep it up!

+ Great job! You are really playing well as a team!

+ That's alright—you will have another chance to score. Keep trying!

+ Nice effort!

+ Way to use what you've learned!

+ Stay with the struggle!

+ Don't let frustration stop you! You can do it!

+ Work together!

+ Give it your best shot!

+ All of your practice shows!

+ Hard work is paying off!

+ Keep up the momentum! You're working together!

+ You are getting stronger!

+ You'll get there!

+ We're proud of your effort!

+ Love that positive attitude!

FIGURE 7.3 CHEERING ON THE SIDELINES SUGGESTIONS

call to the young players, he did not consider what message the fixed time requirements might send to those who had already surpassed the goal. Unlike Colsh's players, who were given a roadmap focused on improvement, Jacob's soccer skills were not expected to grow over the summer.

MHS BOYS SOCCER SKILLS PRE-TEST

Player: _____

Outside right foot dribble (secs.)	Outside left foot dribble (secs.)	Inside right foot dribble (secs.)	Inside left foot dribble (secs.)
Right foot low target/10	Left foot low target/10	Right foot chip high target/10	Left foot chip high target/10

FIGURE 7.4 SOCCER SKILLS FEEDBACK FORM

Colsh readily admitted that being a growth mindset-focused coach can be a challenge and has forced reflection and growth on the part of the coaching staff. "It took us 4 years to get to the assessment of skills piece," Colsh said to us, when asked about the work he and Welch put into the May feedback drills. "Tryouts are a new start for everyone, even if they have played for us before." When players don't make the team, the cuts are often harder on parents than they are for kids, Colsh noted:

> There are so many kids trying out. Your kid could be a star on one team and not make the cut on another. This creates a mindset issue. One of the worst things that we can do in youth sports is identifying standout players too early. It often doesn't mean anything and sets up fixed mindsets in both parents and players.

Jeff Colsh's point is an important one for supportive adults to ponder. Often, children with passions in sports and the arts have their sights set on achievement at the highest levels, earning a college scholarship, or winning a prestigious competition. This focus sometimes comes are the expense of other interests or hobbies. We must help our kids temper these goals. Educational scientist Dr. Pedro de Bruyckere recently said, "Never tell someone to just 'follow your passion.' Follow your passion *and* have something on the side to give you a mental buffer to deal with setbacks" (de Bruyckere, 2022). Colsh's growth mindset orientation helped lead to phenomenal success on the field. Middletown High School's soccer team won the state championship for the first time in 22 years under the leadership of Colsh and Welch.

IF YOU'RE GOING TO MAKE A MISTAKE, MAKE A "DOOZY"

Kearney Francis Blandamer coached field hockey for more than 20 years. For the last five of those, Blandamer was varsity coach at Thomas S. Wootton High School in Rockville, MD, and led her team to an overall 5-year win-loss-tie record of 67-12-1. Along with her sister, junior varsity coach Lesley Francis Stroot, Blandamer took her team to the next level through the deliberate infusion of growth mindset principles into their preparation, feedback, and team philosophy.

Because both Blandamer and Stroot taught at Wootton, they saw the community through a learning lens. They started their mindset journey by reading about Dweck's work and considering its application to the girls at Wootton, an unusually high-achieving community, where the culture of success is bred with vigor. Blandamer admitted to us that,

> From an outsider's perspective, this sounds like a positive thing. They succeed at just about everything they attempt. But this is actually quite crippling. It makes the stakes for failure very high, and actually discourages the highest risk taking. Our students have very high levels of anxiety, and report burnout and early "retirement" from many activities they once enjoyed.

In her first few years at Wootton, Blandamer noticed that her players' fear of failure held them back in tight, high-pressure situations. She was determined to build a culture in which players were comfortable taking risks:

> We need to teach and reinforce the growth mindset. We try to give the girls experiences that get them comfortable being uncomfortable, but now we explain that all we are after is learning. We talk about risk-taking and experiencing challenges and how only when we are uncomfortable can we grow.

To that end, Blandamer and Stroot sought opportunities for their team to play top-ranked teams in the Mid-Atlantic, games that would challenge them beyond the confines of their region.

It was at one of these contests against a top-ranked team that the previously undefeated Wootton girls lost 5-0. Blandamer could not have been more pleased with her team, and the value of growth mindset was more evident than ever:

> My girls were exhausted, banged up, and in an unfamiliar place (being shut out and outscored by such a wide differential). And yet, they talked about having fun, and learning, and the joy of being challenged and tested in a way I have never heard them talk about it before. My team was light, optimistic, and proud after their effort. I've honestly never seen such a transformation.

How did Blandamer and Stroot do it? First, they didn't ask for mistake-free games. In fact, at one halftime huddle, Blandamer told her players the story of Billie Jean King, tennis great, who said, "Be bold. If you are going to make an error, make a doozy." Blandamer's message was that she wanted her players to stop hesitating, be "all in," and learn from any mistakes. John Wooden, famed UCLA basketball coach who led his team to 10 NCAA championships, did not ask for mistake-free games, either. According to Dweck, Wooden didn't demand that his players never lose. He asked for full effort from them. "Did I win? Did I lose?" These are the wrong questions. The correct question is, "Did

I make my best effort?" If so, Wooden said, "You may be outscored, but you *will never lose*" (Dweck, 2006, p. 207). Like Wooden, Blandamer and Stroot focused on players' learning and improvement.

Blandamer was an animated coach on the sidelines, but her messages during the game remained grounded in a growth mindset. For example, her words, "Look at that freshman, Wootton! Look at how hard she's working!" highlighted the extraordinary effort of a young and inexperienced player who nonetheless contributed mightily to the team's performance. Upon taking a player out of the game, Blandamer said to her, "Do you know why I took you out?" The focus, even when providing correction or direction, was always on learning and growing. Wootton's players repeated the language they heard from their coaches, and the culture of growth led Wootton's field hockey team all the way to the state championship game in 2015.

> *The focus, even when providing correction or direction, is always on learning and growing.*

In October 2015, the team was highlighted by *The Washington Post* under the headline "Wootton Continues to Grow." The article referenced the growth mindset of senior Marisa Morakis:

Two years ago, Wootton field hockey suffered its first and only loss of the fall in the Maryland 4A state championship game. Inadequacy and failure do not shape Coach Kearney Blandamer's memory of the event.

What she remembers is the moment after the game, while Severna Park was busy celebrating its 21st state title, when young sophomore Marisa Morakis was defiantly content, crystallizing a philosophy Blandamer had been chasing for years.

The coach has done her homework on excellence. She studied Vince Lombardi and John Wooden. But the tenet she has come to accept as gospel—the one driven into the Patriots' collective psyche every day—is the core thesis of a Stanford psychologist named Carol Dweck. When Morakis approached Blandamer in the minutes after their 2013 season ended, she was displaying a growth mindset.

"She said, 'I worked as hard as I could,'" Blandamer said Morakis told her. "'There is not another thing I could have done.'" And she was happy.

Two years later, Morakis is a senior committed to Bucknell who leads the team with 14 assists. The third-ranked Patriots are the best team in Montgomery County. By eschewing a fixed mindset that would label them a successful team, Wootton isn't particularly pleased with that.

"If you praise ability, the understanding is I can't get any better because that's who I am," Blandamer said. "If you praise effort instead of the ability, the potential for growth is exponential."

"The score doesn't always reflect the amount of learning and the skill of each team," Morakis said. "I think that it's important that we don't get too confident."

(Kasinitz & Hiatt, 2015, paras 10–16)

TIPS FOR COACHES

Parents are often recruited to coach their children's sports teams, whether for pee-wee soccer season or a decade of Little League. Simple concepts like how to organize a team or teach basic techniques and skills can be daunting enough for a newly recruited parent coach, but how can the concept of growth mindset be integrated into the experience? Coaches like Blandamer, Colsh, Stroot, and Welch didn't just accidentally guide their teams to develop a growth mindset about performance. They made deliberate decisions about the ways that they would foster an environment focused on forward momentum and growth. Here are a few of the things they did that could be applied to a variety of coaching situations:

- *Require everyone's best effort.* This means understanding where the "learning zone" is for each player and adjusting instruction to make sure that no one has a walk in the park, but no one is climbing Mt. Everest, either. This also means that it is a waste of breath to praise "hard work" if someone isn't giving his or her best effort.

- *Plan for purposely challenging situations.* Expose players to complex plays, create opportunities to watch and learn from seasoned players with strong skills, and try unique drills that allow for exposure to scenarios where players will make mistakes. Spend time after the drill or experience to discuss what worked well, what could be improved, and what skills need to be addressed next as the team continues to grow.

- *Praise risk-taking.* Having a growth mindset means knowing that sometimes mistakes will be made, but players need to learn to confidently take calculated chances.

- *Frame failures within the context of learning.* Children see failure as a temporary setback when it is discussed as a step in the learning process. Setting aside time to revisit pivotal plays and discuss alternate strategies or examine how another player may have handled the scenario is valuable.

- *Explain the concept of mindsets to the players.* Whether you use a very simple explanation for preschoolers ("We're growing our brains today as we learn how to run the bases!") or a sophisticated one with teenagers ("Remember how we talked about strengthening our neural connections? We're doing that today with this drill"), language and examples from neuroscience can help to reinforce why having a growth mindset is important in athletics.

- *Share the growth mindset message with spectators.* Inform other parents of the environment being built and reinforced for the team. Encourage supportive praise from the sidelines rather than a running commentary of directions.

- ✦ *Celebrate as players grow.* Notice and draw attention to increases in speed, agility, and technique that are the result of practice. Let the team know which players (on the team or in the history of the sport) embody a growth mindset and strong work ethic.
- ✦ *Enlist the help of others.* Capitalize on the power of a shared approach by enlisting the help of other coaches and parents. Hand them this book! If you don't have connections in your own area, dive into online support. One of our favorites is Trevor Ragan's *Train Ugly* website to help make practice more meaningful: https://thelearnerlab.com/train-ugly/

FALL DOWN SEVEN TIMES, STAND UP EIGHT

An old Japanese saying, "fall down seven times, stand up eight" embodies the indomitable spirit that helps our children to happily navigate performance in the arts and in athletics. As parents, we are powerful examples of how important it is to address weaknesses and jump back into the fray. Elite competitions, whether they are for photography or ski jumping, require a strong desire to address weaknesses and learn. Look at the television coverage of the Olympic Games for a great example. Post event, athletes are often asked to critique their performances. Often, these athletes focus on the technical aspects of their performance and suggest what they will do next to improve. This focus on learning and improvement is a hallmark of growth mindset thinking.

> *A focus on learning and improvement is a hallmark of growth mindset thinking.*

Setbacks in athletics or in arts performances or exhibitions, as difficult as they may be for our children (and for us!), are simply a reminder to get back to work.

REFERENCES

Aiello, R. & Sloboda, J. (1994). *Musical perceptions.* New York, NY: Oxford University Press.

Bruser, M. (1999). *The art of practicing: A guide to making music from the heart.* New York, NY: Bell Tower.

Chua, J. (2015). The role of social support in dance talent development. *Journal for the Education of the Gifted, 38,* 169–195.

Colvin, G. (2008). *Talent is overrated: What really separates world-class performers from everybody else.* New York, NY: Portfolio.

De Bruyckere, P. (2022) Shared in online speaking engagement for The Center for Transformative Teaching & Learning, 2 November 2022.

Dweck, C. (2006). *Mindset: The new psychology of success.* New York, NY: Random House.

Kasinitz, A. & Hiatt, G. (2015, October 14). Field hockey: Overtime is no sweat for George Mason; Wootton continues to grow. *The Washington Post.* Retrieved April 10, 2023 from www.washingtonpost.com/sports/highschools/field-hockey-overtime-is-no-sweat-for-george-mason-wootton-continues-to-grow/2015/10/14/78c55bb6-727e-11e5-9cbb-790369643cf9_story.html

Lythcott-Haims, J. (2015). *How to raise an adult: Break free of the overparenting trap and prepare your kid for success.* New York, NY: Henry Holt.

Margiotta, M. (2011). Parental support in the development of young musicians: A teacher's perspective from a small-scale study of piano students and their parents. *Australian Journal of Music Education, 1,* 16–30.

McPherson, G. & Davidson, J. (2002). Musical practice: Mother and child interactions during the first year of learning an instrument. *Music Education Research, 4,* 141–156.

O'Sullivan, J. (2015). *Why kids quit sports.* Retrieved on April 10, 2023 from https://changingthegameproject.com/why-kids-quit-sports/

Rosenwald, M. (2015, October 4). Are parents ruining youth sports? Fewer kids play amid pressure. *The Washington Post.* Retrieved April 10, 2023 from www.washingtonpost.com/local/are-parents-ruining-youth-sports-fewer-kids-play-amid-pressure/2015/10/04/eb1460dc-686e-11e5-9ef3-fed182507eac_story.html

Ross, A. (2006, July 24). The storm of style: Listening to the complete Mozart. *The New Yorker.* Retrieved April 10, 2023 from www.newyorker.com/magazine/2006/07/24/the-storm-of-style

Yocom, G. (2010). My shot: Gary Player. *Golf Digest.* Retrieved April 10, 2023 from www.golfdigest.com/story/myshot_gd0210

CHAPTER 8

WHAT ARE SOME GROWTH MINDSET EXPERIENCES THAT I CAN TRY AT HOME?

"I've seen a different attitude about learning in my daughter since we've focused on mindset at home."

—Amy, parent of two

The first seven chapters may have provided you with a lot to think about. You may be wondering if you have enough perseverance to build a growth mindset home environment (you do!). Take the information and ideas that you have read about and embed them into everyday living. Making an announcement like, "Come into the kitchen! We are all going to talk about mindsets!" would probably not go over well. Instead, work the language into everyday conversation. A great time to do this is right before bedtime when we read books to our elementary age children. Thinking about the characters in some of the books, use books as a vehicle for discussion. What if The Little Engine couldn't?

- ✦ What if the character did not persevere, how would the story be different?
- ✦ Why didn't the character give up?
- ✦ What strategies did the character use?
- ✦ Do you think the character showed growth mindset thinking? Why? How did the character face his mistakes and failures?

DOI: 10.4324/9781003405931-9

You could apply some of the above questions to many books that are probably on your child's shelf or in their book basket right now. Figure 8.1 is a list of specific books that allow for discussion about mindsets. A sample question or two is also provided, but feel free to come up with your own questions to get your children thinking.

Title	Author	Character	Mindset	Some Questions to Ask Your Child About the Book
			Picture Books	
A Little Bit of Oomph!	Barney Saltzberg	N/A	Growth	What does "oomph" mean? Why does the author think that the things in the book (like seeds) need a little oomph? Why is oomph important for a growth mindset?
Almost	Richard Torrey	Jack	Growth	How is the word almost similar to the word yet?
Beautiful Oops!	Barney Saltzberg	NA	Growth	Why did the author write this book? What can we learn about mistakes after reading this? What are some ways that we can turn a mistake into something positive?
Bounce Back! A Book About Resilience	Cheri J. Meiners	The girl	Growth	What does it mean when someone says he or she is going to "bounce back"?
Dream Big, Little Pig!	Kristi Yamaguchi	Poppy	Growth	Poppy dreams about being a dancer, singer, and a model. What stands in her way of reaching these dreams (practice, effort)? Why does Poppy finally succeed in learning to ice skate?
Everyone Can Learn to Ride a Bicycle	Chris Raschka	The child	Growth	What are some of the things that the child tried when she was learning to ride the bike? What are some words that describe the child?
Giraffes Can't Dance	Gile Andreae and Guy Parker-Rees	Gerald	Both	Why did Gerald change his mind about his own dancing abilities?
Penelope Perfect: A Tale of Perfectionism Gone Wild	Shannon Anderson	Penelope	Fixed, then Growth	At the beginning of the story, Penelope did everything perfectly. Why do you think being perfect was important to her?
Mirette on the High Wire	Emily Arnold McCully	Mirette	Growth	Describe Mirette's mindset. How did she learn to walk across the rope?
Matthew's Dream	Leo Lionni	Matthew	Growth	Once Matthew decided to become a painter, what did he do to become a famous painter?
Making a Splash	Carol E. Riley	Lisa and Johnny	Lisa = Growth Johnny = Fixed	What did Lisa do when she felt herself sinking? What did she learn from this experience?
The Most Magnificent Thing	Ashley Spires	Girl	Growth	Why didn't the little girl just give up?
Odd Boy Out: Young Albert Einstein	Don Brown	Albert	Growth	Why did Albert's teacher tell him that he will "never get anywhere in life"? What are some ways that Albert demonstrated a growth mindset?
Rosie Revere, Engineer	Andrea Beaty	Rosie and Great, Great Aunt Rose	Aunt Rose = Growth	Why did the children stand and cheer for each failure?
Ruby's Wish	Shirin Yim Bridges	Ruby	Growth	Why did Ruby's grandfather allow her to attend university? What was his mindset?

FIGURE 8.1 GROWTH MINDSET BOOKS

Source: Ricci (2020, p. 138). Reprinted with permission.

Title	Author	Character	Mindset	Some Questions to Ask Your Child About the Book
Someday	Eileen Spinelli	Little girl	Growth	What kinds of things is the little girl doing to prepare for the things she wants to do someday?
Stuck	**Oliver Jeffers**	Floyd	Growth	Why didn't Floyd just give up?
Thank You, Mr. Falker	Patricia Polacco	Trisha	Fixed, then growth	**What are some ways that Trisha had a fixed mindset?**
Walk On! A Guide for Babies of All Ages	Marla Frazee	Baby	Growth	How is learning to walk the same as learning with a growth mindset?
Wilma Unlimited	Kathleen Krull	Wilma Rudolph	Growth	What are some ways that Wilma persevered through her hardships?
Chapter Books				
Charlie and the Chocolate Factory	Roald Dahl	Charlie	Growth	Did Willy Wonka have a growth mindset, fixed mindset, or both? Explain why.
Fish in a Tree	Lynda Mullaly Hunt	Ally	Growth	On page 239, Mr. Daniels said to his class: "In fact, all of these people had grit to spare." What does he mean?
Flutter: The Story of Four Sisters and an Incredible Journey	Erin E. Moulton	Maple	Growth	Maple and Dawn demonstrate a growth mindset when they are on their journey. Did they make the right decision? What are some other examples of when having a growth mindset might lead to a dangerous situation?
Holes	Louis Sachar	Warden, Mr. Sir, Mr. Pendanski	Fixed	In some ways, the adults had a growth mindset—they **were determined to find the treasure and the Warden was** willing to have the boys dig for years until the treasure was **found. Give examples of the fixed mindset behaviors that the adults exhibited. How is it possible to have both a fixed** and growth mindset?
The Miraculous Journey of Edward Tulane	Kate DiCamillo	Edward	Both	Why does Edward's mindset change? What changed inside of Edward during his life?
Wonder	R. J. Palacio	Summer	Growth	**Would you describe Summer as having a fixed or growth** mindset? Find evidence from the text to support your response.

FIGURE 8.1 CONTINUED

THINGS TO LOOK FOR IN A GROWTH MINDSET HOME

If we walked into your home and spent some time with your family, would we know it was a growth mindset environment? What would we hear? What might we see? What are some things that family members might be doing?

Things we might see include:

+ papers displayed that show growth, improvement, and effort (not all "A" papers);
+ children and parents working hard;
+ games/puzzles that stretch thinking;
+ optimistic viewpoints; and
+ resiliency in the face of setbacks.

Things we might hear include:

+ "You don't quite understand yet."
+ "Great effort!"
+ "I noticed a lot of improvement."
+ "You have really grown in that area."
+ "I see you have used a lot of different strategies!"

Things we might see you do include:

+ appreciate processes more than outcomes;
+ value work ethic;
+ stay calm and growth mindset oriented when a child brings home a less than stellar grade or report card; and
+ set age-appropriate goals with your children.

Growth mindset homes might also include visual reminders for children to encourage them to change their thinking, including pictures or posters of role models who have persevered and succeeded, or putting up quotes about failure and trying again. Other materials, like the growth mindset poster in Appendix C, can be hung in your child's room or study area as a trigger for thinking about having a growth mindset. (But remember, it's not enough just to hang up the poster!)

GROWTH MINDSET MOMENTS FOR OUR TODDLERS AND PRE-K KIDS

Every day we must take advantage of opportunities for our children to develop a growth mindset. This is particularly important to do with our toddlers and preschool-age children. We must allow them to assert their independence and learn that it is okay if things don't come easily. In chapter 1, we shared data that showed that 100% of students entering kindergarten displayed a growth mindset, but by the time they reached third grade, 42% of these students had a fixed mindset when it came to learning in school. Strengthening growth mindset thinking as toddlers and preschoolers will help our kids maintain growth mindset thinking as they progress through school.

Let's look at a few scenarios that provide parents with opportunities to reinforce a growth mindset message.

Four-year-old Noelle was putting on her coat and realized that she could not get her arm in her sleeve (her hat and mittens were in there). Grandma noticed that she was becoming frustrated and ran over to help her just as Noelle's mom Patrice was entering the room. Patrice intercepted Grandma and asked Noelle what was happening. Patrice gently reminded Noelle that her hat and mittens were in the sleeve (Noelle probably already knew this) and asked her how she might fix the situation. Patrice did not solve the problem for her. Instead, she provided an opportunity for her daughter to persist until she was able to remove the barrier in the sleeve, and successfully put on her coat.

This situation portrays a growth mindset moment. It is often easier just to quickly solve minor issues ourselves because it is a fast way to calm a frustrated child. Add to that the morning rush when we sometimes have no time to spare, and you have a recipe that creates the tendency to quickly solve problems for our kids: "I will get your shoes," or "Let me do that for you." But what message does that send to your child? Messages like this: "I don't think you can help yourself, so I will do it for you." Teaching our toddlers and preschool-age children that struggle is an important part of learning and growing will serve them well as they grow. It sometimes takes patience on the part of the adults. Give children the time that they need to develop these skills.

Think about this scenario:

Cain received a 3D dinosaur bones puzzle for his birthday. Cain loves dinosaurs. As soon as he saw this gift, he stopped opening his other gifts and began working on the puzzle. With great excitement, he dumped the dinosaur bones on the floor and began assembling the bones. He glanced at the picture of the dinosaur on the box as he worked. Within 10 minutes he had perfectly assembled the puzzle. His father exclaimed, "That's my boy! He is so super smart! Look what he was able to do with no help from anyone! Isn't he just the smartest boy around?" Cain was beaming as his mom and other family members nodded in agreement.

Dad is happy, Mom is happy, Cain is happy. So, what could possibly be wrong? The issue is that this was a missed opportunity for a growth mindset moment. What are some possible growth mindset responses that could have occurred? What could have been said to Cain after he built his 3D dinosaur? How could this have become a growth mindset moment?

Jot possible responses here:

_____

_____

_____

_____

_____

_____

_____

_____

_____

_____

_____

_____

_____

_____

_____

_____

_____

_____

_____

_____

_____

If you are reading this as part of a book club or with a friend, talk about the responses you wrote on the previous page. If not, reflect on your own. Do they speak to Cain's process or just the outcome? Do your responses value effort and the strategy he used? Does it matter how quickly Cain put the puzzle together? (No, it does not.) Your responses should value Cain's process or the strategy that he used and his persistence or effort. Looking at the puzzle box to see what the dinosaur should look like when it is completed was one of Cain's visible strategies. Try to imagine what message Cain hears in each of the responses. How might those messages impact his own thinking about his ability and what his parents value? How might those messages influence Cain's ability to persist the next time he encounters a new puzzle that is more challenging?

VIDEO DISCUSSIONS FOR PRESCHOOL KIDS

A few videos that our young children can view include:

✦ *You Can Learn Anything* (www.youtube.com/watch?v=JC82Il2c jqA)—This one-and-a-half-minute video reminds kids that we all start at "zero"—that learning sometimes involves struggle and frustration but with persistence, we can learn anything.

✦ *A Secret About the Brain* (www.youtube.com/watch?v=lz49YsEV cb4)—Mojo learns a secret from his friend Katie that changes how he thinks about learning!

✦ *The Magic of Mistakes* (www.youtube.com/watch?v=aJwjH0S4 V_k)—Mojo enters a robotics competition and wins an unexpected prize: a new mindset!

✦ *Sesame Street: Bruno Mars: Don't Give Up* (www.youtube.com/ watch?v=pWp6kkz-pnQ)—Bruno Mars sings about not giving up.

✦ *Zootopia: Shakira: Try Anything* (www.youtube.com/watch?v= LnSYihRoGA4)—This is a short music video (from a full-length Disney film) about overcoming mistakes and trying new things every day.

We also love this animated short:

✦ *Soar* by Alice Tzue (www.youtube.com/watch?v=UUlaseGr kLc&list=PLkAVUURATZSe51t6LzZxPd0H8-bpB088N)

There are a lot of opportunities for your child to interpret the film since there is no dialogue. Ask questions like:

✦ How do they feel after they fail?
✦ What strategies does she use when she is helping the pilot?

Watch these with your kids and talk to them about what they learned from each video. Ask them how they can use the information that they learned.

Consider this scenario about Ryan and his dad:

Almost 13-year-old Ryan couldn't wait to turn 13, the age when his parents would purchase a cell phone for him to use! When his dad came home with the new phone, Ryan couldn't wait to get his hands on it and set it up. Even though he knew that the phone technically belonged to his parents, Ryan was excited to set it up like his friends' phones. Just as Ryan thought his dad was going to hand him the box, his dad took out the phone and proclaimed that he would set it up for him "the right way." Ryan insisted that he could figure it out and wanted to set it up. Dad disagreed and said that Ryan didn't have the experience to do it and continued to set it up, chose ringtones and download apps that he though Ryan needed.

What just happened? Perhaps dad didn't want Ryan to get frustrated, or he was afraid that Ryan would not do it correctly, or maybe he just enjoys setting up new phones. Whatever the reason, what message did this action send to Ryan?

Maybe Ryan would have struggled while he was learning the ins and outs of setting up a new phone. That's great! That struggle would allow him to try different strategies, learn from mistakes and persevere! This was a missed opportunity for growth mindset thinking. If Ryan and his dad had set up the phone together, they might have been able to coach each other through frustration using growth mindset thinking!

MY GROWTH MINDSET GOALS

Name: _____ Date: _____

I want to be able to _____

_____.

Right now I can _____

_____,

but I need to learn how to_____

_____

and practice _____

_____.

Draw a picture of yourself working to reach your goal.

Check In:
❑ Goal met and ready for a new goal!
❑ I'm still working hard on this one!

FIGURE 8.2 MY GROWTH MINDSET GOAL (PRIMARY VERSION)

Source: Ricci (2020, p. 138). Reprinted with permission.

MY GROWTH MINDSET GOALS

Name: ___Josephine___   Date: ___April 1___

I want to be able to <u>set the table for dinner by myself</u>
_____ .

Right now I can <u>get the silverware and help my brother set</u>
<u>the table</u> _____ ,

but I need to learn how to <u>put the plates, knives, forks, and</u>
<u>spoons in the right places at the table</u> _____

and practice <u>placing the utensils around the plates correctly</u>
_____ .

Draw a picture of yourself working to reach your goal.

Check In:
❑ Goal met and ready for a new goal!
☑ I'm still working hard on this one!

FIGURE 8.3 SAMPLE: MY GROWTH MINDSET GOAL

Source: Ricci (2020, p. 138). Reprinted with permission.

MY GROWTH MINDSET GOAL

Name: _____ Date: _____

Growth Mindset Goal: _____
_____

I hope to reach my goal by: _____

Strategies or things I might do to help reach my goal:
_____
_____

Check-In:
How am I doing toward this Growth Mindset Goal? Date: _____
❑ I have met this goal   ❑ I have partially met this goal
❑ I have not met this goal yet

An example of something I did that made me realize that I have met, have partially met, or have not yet met this goal:
_____
_____
_____
_____

Some new strategies to try or my new growth mindset goal:
_____
_____
_____
_____

(If you have a new goal, get a blank Growth Mindset Goal form.)

FIGURE 8.4 MY GROWTH MINDSET GOAL (OLDER CHILDREN)
Source: Ricci (2020, p. 138). Reprinted with permission.

Finally, let's think about 16-year-old Lexi:

Lexi was excited about summer break from school so that she could get a job. She really wanted to start saving her money so that she could get a used car when she graduated from high school. She went online and began applying to many jobs: fast food, retail, summer camps, you name it. When she didn't get any responses, her mother suggested that she write letters to the managers to tell them about herself and why she would be good at the job. Lexi did not think this was a good idea. She told her mom, "That's not what people do now." Mom noticed that Lexi was becoming discouraged, so she decided that she would write a few letters so that Lexi could just sign her name and mail them. When mom presented the letters to her, Lexi became angry! "I can handle it myself," she protested. Lexi continued to apply to jobs with no luck.

This scenario is a tricky one. On one hand, Lexi wanted to handle the process herself, which demonstrates her increasing responsibility as a young adult. When her first attempts were not successful, however, she didn't change her strategy for getting a job. She simply continued to complete the online applications and wait for something to happen. Even though she was not successful, what could Lexi learn from this? What kinds of questions could she ask herself as she reflects on her perceived failure to get a job?

Lexi's mom was trying to help move the process along, but by writing letters for Lexi, she fell into a parenting trap—over-helping.
Could Lexi have:

✦ Walked around her town or the local mall to introduce herself to the store manager?
✦ Put flyers in mailboxes in her neighborhood, or hang a flyer in her apartment building offering babysitting services, doing odd jobs or running errands?
✦ Asked a parent or trusted adult to review her resume?
✦ Included a few references from teachers or neighbors?

As parents, it is helpful to avoid saying things like, "I told you that you should have sent letters," and instead, promote reflection with conversation starters like, "Let's come up with some ideas that would help get your application noticed next time." We can also share the challenges that we had getting our first job.

GOAL SETTING

Setting goals with your children is another way to help your children build a growth mindset. Figure 8.2 is an example goal-setting form that you might use with younger children. Talk to your child about something that she might want to learn to do, what her starting point is, and some ways that she can reach her goal. Fill in the form with your child, not for them. Ask them to think about each part carefully as it is completed. Figure 8.3 includes a sample goal-setting form to help you with this process. Your child can then draw a picture of themself reaching their goal—this helps children visualize the goal.

Figure 8.4 is a goal-setting form that can be used with older children, helping them set goals specifically focused on building their own growth mindset. They, too, might want to create an image of themselves reaching their goals—perhaps through drawing a picture, making a collage, or visualizing and thinking about how they might look and feel when their achievement is reached.

GROWTH MINDSET "ADVENTURES"

Another way to reinforce growth mindset thinking is to take advantage of opportunities that provide chances to model and coach kids through new and unfamiliar experiences. These chances are around every corner if we take the time to keep our eyes and ears open and if we are careful not to allow our own fixed mindset thinking to creep in. Let's consider a possible scenario.

> At the library, Luis, father of two, noticed a poster advertising an upcoming birdhouse-making workshop for families at the local community center. Two thoughts came into his head simultaneously:
> "My kids, Ethan and Nora, would love to do this! They enjoy feeding the birds and they would love learning how to make a birdhouse."
> "I can't hammer a nail straight into a piece of wood. There is no way I can make a birdhouse, especially not in front of a lot of people ... especially in front of my kids."

This is an experience that has the potential to be a family growth mindset adventure. Luis will be learning alongside his children as they follow the instructions to complete the birdhouse project. Ethan and Nora will learn new skills and have the chance to practice perseverance and resiliency. Luis will have authentic opportunities to use growth mindset feedback and praise.

Most importantly, while it may be uncomfortable for him at first and he might feel worried or frustrated about the outcome, Luis can be an example of growth mindset thinking to his children as he shows them how he can learn something new and gain increasing confidence in his woodworking ability. Modeling our own productive struggle to learn something new or gain confidence in an area where we are not proficient is one of the very best ways in which we can help children see the growth mindset in action.

Growth mindset adventures are possible in so many situations when you take the time to look for them. We've included just a few examples here.

You might take your family on a weekend hike made more challenging by the recent snowfall. When you promised that Saturday was the day for the hike, you didn't know it would snow. You have a choice: Cancel the hike or embrace the challenge and tell the family that this will be a new adventure! Bundle up, put on your boots, and head out. Will it be more challenging? Yes. Will you have to make modifications to your plan? Sure. Will you have lots of opportunities to talk your kids through challenges and obstacles? You bet!

Your neighbors ask you to go camping with them for the weekend even though you grew up in the city and don't know the first thing about camping. You have a choice. Politely decline the offer or take a risk and accept the offer to borrow their extra tent and sleeping bags. It is likely that you'll have to ask your neighbors for help or advice as you struggle to pitch the tent. You might experience some frustration as you try to get a fire started. Each of these is a growth mindset moment. You can "think out loud" as you talk yourself through the adventure and you can ask you kids to help you learn. What a powerful message about the importance of lifelong growth and learning.

You want to rent two bicycles to ride with your child at the beach and the rental stand has only one bike left … and it is a tandem bike (one built for two people). The vendor apologizes and offers you a discount, but you've never ridden a tandem bike before. You have a choice. Forget the bike idea altogether or go for it and try the tandem bike. The tandem bike will feel awkward at first. It will test your patience. It will probably also result in one of the funny stories told in your family history for years to come—but it is also an opportunity for a growth mindset adventure.

It might also be a missed opportunity at home—perhaps you avoid the crossword puzzle in the Sunday paper because you may not think you will have success with it. Let your kids know that you have avoided it in the past but now, with your fresh, new mindset you are going to give it a try and not give up. If you end up needing support, share some of the strategies that you might use to help you with it. You don't have to be successful—what your kids will see is that you are not afraid to try.

One area of caution: It is important that your kids know that having an "I can do it" attitude should not be applied to every situation. It could sometimes lead to a potentially harmful outcome. For example, a child might need a ride after school or another event. Instead of calling home for a ride, the child thinks, "I know my way home. I know I can walk there without getting lost." The perseverance that a child is willing to exercise in a case like this is misguided. Be sure to discuss situations like this with your child.

Growth mindset moments can happen every day. We must purposefully react to everyday situations in a deliberate way to foster resilience, model perseverance, and ensure that our children see a growth mindset as part of our daily life.

REFERENCE

Ricci, M. (2020). *Ready-to-use resources for mindsets in the classroom: Everything educators need for school success.* Waco, TX: Prufrock Press.

FINAL THOUGHTS

Parenting advice is a regular topic on the morning television shows, in magazines, and on social media. The myriad of "dos and don'ts" is easily overwhelming and many times one piece of advice contradicts another. It can be confusing and frustrating. It is likely that you have also heard advice from your relatives and other friends who are parents. We recognize that parents bring unique perspectives to the important work of raising children and know that each of you needs to filter all the messages and advice and determine what is best for your family.

The concept of mindsets, and the power of instilling growth mindset thinking in children, has proven to be a very powerful influence on both of us and the children that we interact with on a regular basis. It has changed the way we approach new learning, the way we praise the children we love, and the way we respond to our own challenges, struggles, and frustrations. As we have shared information about fixed and growth mindset thinking, neuroplasticity, resiliency, and perseverance with others, they have repeatedly said things like, "This makes so much sense when I think of it in relation to my son!", and "I wish I could go back and change some of the ways I responded to my own children's struggles," and "My life would have been different if I had not given up so quickly on my dream of being a scientist because I thought I was not smart enough." These are just a few of the many reasons we wrote this book.

DOI: 10.4324/9781003405931-10

The concept of mindsets, and the power of instilling a growth mindset in children, has proven to be a very powerful influence on both of us and the children who we interact with on a regular basis. It has changed the way we approach new learning, the way we praise the children we love, and the way we respond to our own challenges, struggles, and frustrations.

We hope that the information shared and the suggestions included in this book will help you to cultivate a growth mindset home for yourself and for your children. Remember, every time you learn something new, you create new neural pathways. You now have a neural pathway about the power of the growth mindset! Strengthen it every day by practicing growth mindset thinking, growth mindset praise, and growth mindset feedback. You can be successful!

ANSWER KEY FOR PARENT MINDSET REFLECTION TOOL

Key: **F** = Fixed, **G** = Growth, **N** = Neutral

1. Your child comes home with an A on his paper. You say:
   a. This is awesome! You are so smart! **(F)**
   b. Good—you know I expect A work from you. **(F)**
   c. Wow! Your studying really paid off. **(G)**
2. Your child comes home with a less-than-desirable grade on a paper. You say:
   a. I told you that you should have spent more time working on this. **(N)**
   b. I don't know why your teacher is such a tough grader. You need to talk to her about this. **(F)**
   c. How did you go about doing this assignment? What might you do differently next time? **(G)**
3. Your child scores the winning point on her team. You say:
   a. I am so proud of you! They won because of you! **(F)**
   b. Wow! All of that practice really paid off! **(G)**
   c. You sure did get lucky. Good for you! **(F)**

4. Your child gets nervous and does not do as well as you expected during a performance or event. You say:
   a. You were terrific! **(F)**
   b. It wasn't your best performance. I could tell you were a little nervous. **(N)**
   c. I can tell you are not happy with your performance. What do you think you can do to be ready for the next time so you will feel more confident? **(G)**

5. You notice that your child is spending a lot of time trying to figure something out (a game, puzzle, app, technology, etc.). You say:
   a. You are working really hard to figure that out. I am glad you haven't given up. **(G)**
   b. I think you have worked on that long enough. Just give up. **(F)**
   c. Here, let me do that for you. **(F)**

6. You notice that your child quits things quickly/gives up. You say:
   a. I am glad that you have interests in so many things. **(N)**
   b. Try to stick with it a little longer, practice, or try a new way to approach it. **(G)**
   c. That's OK. I want to give up when things get tough, too. **(F)**

7. Your typically high-achieving child is not performing well in a particular subject. In fact, you notice that things are getting worse. How do you react?
   a. You try to find out how others are performing in this particular class. Perhaps it is the way the teacher is presenting new information? **(F)**
   b. You let your child know what the consequences (technology grounding, limited social events) will be if he doesn't show improvement quickly. **(F)**
   c. You talk with your child to try to figure out what is getting in the way of his learning (confusion, distraction, pace, etc.) and what might help him succeed. **(G)**

8. You notice that your child is struggling with a task. You:
   a. Distract her with a different task. **(F)**
   b. Let her know that struggle is OK. **(G)**
   c. Help her with the task. **(F)**
9. You notice that your child avoids a challenging situation (such as a game, a sport or an academic class). When you ask why, he states that it is "stupid." Your reaction to this observation:
   a. Ask why he thinks it is stupid and listen for fixed mindset thinking. **(N)**
   b. Tell him that he doesn't have to put himself in these situations—just do what he is comfortable with. **(F)**
   c. Let him know that it is OK if he can't do it yet. **(G)**
10. Your child gets angry when he makes a careless mistake. You:
    a. Tell him to settle down and not get mad. **(N)**
    b. Share a story about when you failed or made a mistake and learned from it. **(G)**
    c. Get angry as well; he knew better. **(F)**

REPLACING FIXED MINDSET STATEMENTS

PARENTS' FIXED MINDSET STATEMENTS

In Figure 3.1 in chapter 3, you read each of the fixed mindset statements that you, as a parent, might say about yourself (in the left column). Then you wrote a replacement statement in the right column. Here are some possible replacement statements that you can use to reflect on your thinking. Remember, our own growth-focused self-talk can help our children to develop a growth mindset.

FIXED MINDSET STATEMENT	GROWTH MINDSET REPLACEMENT STATEMENT
I am a terrible cook!	*I need to find some videos online that demonstrate some of these cooking techniques that I can't do yet.*
I will never be good at that.	*I have a long way to go to become good at that, but I will get there if I keep working at it!*
I have a green thumb.	*I have learned a lot about plants over the years. I am always looking for new techniques and information to increase my knowledge.*
I leave that (finance, technology, cooking, etc.) to my partner.	*I don't always take care of the (bills, computer, meal preparation) but I am sure that with practice I could do it.*
You can't teach an old dog new tricks.	*It is important to be a lifelong learner and to try new things.*

PARENT TO CHILD FIXED MINDSET STATEMENTS

In Figure 3.2 in chapter 3, you read each of the fixed mindset statements that you, as a parent, might say to your child (in the left column) and wrote at least one growth mindset statement that could replace the fixed mindset statement. Let's look at some possible growth mindset replacement statements. Remember, your words have a powerful impact on your child's own mindset development.

FIXED MINDSET STATEMENT	GROWTH MINDSET REPLACEMENT STATEMENT
You are so smart!	*I can see how much effort you put into your work!*
You are "gifted." You should know how to do this.	*Think about what you already know about this. What else do you need to learn to complete the task?*
Math wasn't my thing either.	*Just because math is challenging for you doesn't mean that you can't master it.*
None of us in this family are good at _____	*None of the rest of us are good at _____ _____, but maybe it is because we didn't have the opportunity to learn and practice.*
You are so lucky; you don't have to study much!	*It seems like this came easily for you. Maybe we can find something more challenging for you to try.*
You are my little artist and your sister is my little author.	*I'm glad that you enjoy working hard on your artwork just like your sister works at her writing.*
This is so easy for you. You don't even have to try!	*If you don't have to put forth any effort, you aren't stretching yourself. Let's see if we can find a way to make it more fun and challenging for you.*

GROWTH MINDSET POSTER

THIS GRAPHIC SHOWS A BRAIN GROWING LIKE A PLANT

Source: M. C. Ricci. (2020). *Ready-to-Use Resources for Mindsets in the Classroom*, 2nd ed. (p. 118). Waco, TX: Prufrock Press. Copyright 2020 by Prufrock Press. Reprinted with permission

DISCUSSION QUESTIONS FOR BOOK CLUB

If you are thinking about gathering some friends together or are considering using this book for a book club at your child's school, in your church, or with your parent group, the following questions might get you started when discussing this book. Keep in mind that the best book discussions are an interesting balance of insights gained from the text and the readers' personal connections to what they read. Some people may be cautious about sharing personal stories or anecdotes—be sure to respect all voices and comfort levels in the group. Pick and choose questions that appeal to your participants or come up with your own discussion starters.

CHAPTER 1

✦ In what facets of your own life do you tend to have a fixed mindset? How has having a fixed mindset in this area affected you?

✦ In what facets of your own life do you tend to have a growth mindset? How has having a growth mindset in this area affected you?

+ Is the idea that intelligence is malleable a new concept for you? Does having this information adjust your perspective in any way? How?
+ What do you hope to learn from the rest of the book?

CHAPTER 2

+ Were you surprised by the results of the parent mindset reflection tool? Why or why not?
+ Would anyone like to share an example of a time when you demonstrated a fixed or growth mindset with your kids?
+ How do you react to failure? Share an example.
+ How do your children respond to seeing you struggle with a task?
+ It is likely that a variety of different mindsets (of both adults and children) exist in your home. What beginning steps might you take to move toward a growth mindset home environment?
+ What sorts of talents/abilities (or lack thereof!) have you heard others connect to heredity? Have you experienced that in your own life?

CHAPTER 3

+ What types of praise and feedback do you hear at your child's school, sporting events, or recitals? Share some examples. How could the language be adjusted (if necessary) to promote a growth mindset?
+ Share a scenario that happened in your household recently where you applied (or could have applied) each type of praise:

+ Process praise
+ Strategy praise
+ Persistence praise

+ When might it be helpful to remind a child of the "power of *yet?*" How might that sound at all levels of a child's development (toddler, child, tween, teenager, young adult)?
+ Let's share some of the replacement statements that you came up with (see Figure 3.1, pp. 52–53).

CHAPTER 4

+ Has learning about neuroplasticity and how the brain works changed your thinking about learning? How?
+ What opportunities might you have to share simple neuroscience concepts with your children?

CHAPTER 5

+ How have psychosocial skills (perseverance, resiliency, grit, etc.) contributed to your success or the success of those you know?
+ Share an example of a time when it was difficult to watch your child struggle or fail. How did you respond? Might you respond differently if it were to happen again?
+ How do parents accept failure without sending a message that suggests tolerance of mediocrity or of less than a child's best effort?

CHAPTER 6

+ What examples of fixed and growth mindset practices have you witnessed in place in your child's education?
+ What are some things that you might be able to do if your child has a teacher who demonstrates fixed mindset thinking and it is becoming detrimental to your child?
+ What ideas or suggestions do you have to help move your child's academic experience in a growth-oriented direction?

CHAPTER 7

+ What opportunities does your child have to engage in practice? Is practice a chore in your home? Why or why not?
+ How can you motivate your child to engage in deliberate practice?
+ How could the use of growth mindset language at sporting events change the experience of the players? How could it change the tone of the game? How could it change the enjoyment of the spectators?

CHAPTER 8

+ Which tools do you think will be the most valuable for your family? How will you use them?
+ What other resources do you know about that promote a growth mindset home environment?

MINDSETS FOR PARENTS REFLECTION EXERCISE

One of the challenges of growth mindset parenting is the fact that life "happens" so fast! Opportunities to provide support and feedback that will help our children to develop a growth mindset are present every day, but they can be easy to miss in the whirlwind of work and school obligations, chores, and errands. At other times, we recognize 2 minutes too late that we missed a valuable opportunity to provide growth mindset praise or ask a question that might have prompted a child to reframe a struggle as a learning opportunity.

These exercises provide a chance to consider some scenarios *before* they happen in your own family. By taking some time to ponder your responses, you can "practice on paper" the kinds of responses that you hope you'll employ when similar situations present themselves. If you are reading this book as part of a book study or with your spouse or parenting partner, you might want to use these scenarios to prompt some discussion and share ideas. Remember, don't look at your answers as *right* or *wrong*; instead, try to think about ways to employ the strategies in this book as you customize the responses to support the development of a growth mindset in your child. The first exercise has been completed as an example.

Scenario:
You just watched your 7-year-old son participate in basketball "try-outs" at the local recreation center. This will be his first year playing basketball on a team, and he has been excited about the try-outs for weeks. Although you know that because this is a recreation league, all of the kids will "make" a team, your son gets in the car very concerned about the fact that he did not make as many baskets as the other kids. "They are so good at basketball, and I'm not," he says to you. "I've changed my mind. I don't think I want to play at all."
Reflect: Things I could ask myself or think to myself about this situation:
✦ He is tired, so having a conversation about the try-outs now is probably not going to be productive. I think I will wait until he's rested and had something to eat before we make any decisions about his future in basketball.   ✦ He hasn't played basketball on a team before, and his only practice has been in the driveway and in P.E. class at school.
Things I might say to foster a growth mindset:
✦ "Which parts of the try-outs were the most challenging? What do you think you can do to improve in those skills?" (Listen for ways to provide support.)   ✦ "Which of your friends have already played basketball on a team? We could invite them over to help you learn the ropes."   ✦ "Being on a basketball team isn't just about making shots. Moving the ball down the court, passing the ball, and setting up the shots are just as important. You'll learn all of these skills from playing on the team."
Actions I might take to foster a growth mindset:
✦ Find opportunities to help your son practice with others and develop his confidence and skills.   ✦ Watch a basketball game with him (on TV or in person) and point out that even experienced players miss shots and make errors. Highlight how they recover from mistakes and keep playing.

Scenario:
For as long as you can remember, your 18-year-old daughter has wanted to be a fashion designer. She has sketched her designs, repurposed her older brother's clothes, and embellished clothing since she was 9 years old. She is now in her first year of college as a fashion design major and you get a call from her saying, "This sewing class is so hard. My professor wants everything done so fast and it takes me longer. I had to redo the pockets three times to get them right. I should have dropped this class."

Reflect: Things I could ask myself or think to myself about this situation:

Things I might say to foster a growth mindset:

Actions I might take to foster a growth mindset:

Scenario:
You have spent the last 3 weeks helping your 5-year-old son learn to tie his shoes. He has made progress toward being able to tie by himself, but he still needs a little help to get the laces tight enough. This morning, your son came home from a visit to his grandmother's house and can't wait to show you the new sneakers she bought him with elastics instead of shoelaces. "Now I don't have to learn how to tie!" he says.
Reflect: Things I could ask myself or think to myself about this situation:
Things I might say to foster a growth mindset:
Actions I might take to foster a growth mindset:

Scenario:

Your 10-year-old daughter has been learning about goal setting in school and recently set a goal to score 100% on each Friday spelling test this month. For the first 2 weeks, she was successful, but this week, she misspelled three words and scored an 85%. She can be a perfectionist and is very upset that she doesn't have a perfect score this week. "I wasted all of that time studying," she says, "and it didn't even pay off!"

Reflect: Things I could ask myself or think to myself about this situation:

Things I might say to foster a growth mindset:

Actions I might take to foster a growth mindset:

Scenario:

Your 13-year-old son is required to give 30 hours of community service for a club that he belongs to. He is struggling to decide what to do and he is looking for the "easiest" service to provide just to get it done. The deadline for completing service is approaching fast. He shares the following with you: "You know when I help you in the yard and help you stuff envelopes for your work? Can I count those hours toward my service requirement? I am so busy and have so much homework it will be impossible for me to get all my hours done in time."

Reflect: Things I could ask myself or think to myself about this situation:

Things I might say to foster a growth mindset:

Actions I might take to foster a growth mindset:

Scenario:

Your hard-working 16-year-old daughter comes home in tears and yells "I hate my friends!" before running to her bedroom and closing the door. You gently knock on the door and sit down on the bed to ask her what is wrong. Her reply: "Report cards came out today, and all of my friends were bragging about making honor roll and their high GPA. They kept asking me what I got and what honor roll I made. They should know by now that I don't learn as fast as they do. I am so frustrated. I even study more than they do!"

Reflect: Things I could ask myself or think to myself about this situation:

Things I might say to foster a growth mindset:

Actions I might take to foster a growth mindset:

ABOUT THE AUTHORS

Mary Cay Ricci is an education consultant, speaker, and author of *The New York Times* best-selling education book, *Mindsets in the Classroom: Building a Growth Mindset Learning Community*; its companion, *Ready-to-Use Resources for Mindsets in the Classroom*; children's book, *Nothing You Can't Do! The Secret Power of Growth Mindsets*, and a book for education administrators, *Create a Growth Mindset School: An Administrator's Guide to Leading a Growth Mindset Community*. She is a former supervisor of the Office of Advanced and Enriched Instruction in Prince George's County Public Schools, Maryland. She was previously the coordinator of gifted and talented education for Baltimore County Public Schools and an instructional specialist in the Division of Accelerated and Enriched Instruction for Montgomery County Public Schools in Maryland. Mary Cay holds an MSc in Education from Johns Hopkins University, where she was previously a faculty associate in the Graduate School of Education. Mary Cay has Pennsylvania roots, having grown up in a suburb of Pittsburgh and completed her undergraduate degree in elementary education at Mercyhurst University in Erie, PA. She has experience as an elementary and middle school teacher. She is mom to three adult children, Christopher, Patrick, and Isabella, and one great pooch, Sadie.

Margaret ("Meg") Lee has been a public-school educator for over 25 years. Meg's experience includes teaching middle school English, serving as a literacy specialist, a district-level professional developer, middle school administrator, and supervisor of advanced academics. She currently serves as director of organizational development for a school system in Maryland. Meg taught courses in education and psychology at the undergraduate and graduate levels and served as a policy advisor on Mind Brain Education Science for the International Society for Technology in Education. Meg's work in the field of the science of learning has led her to collaborative projects with the Center for Transformative Teaching & Learning, Alliance for Excellent Education, the Education Writers Association, and the Chan Zuckerberg Initiative. She has written for *EdSurge*, *Impact: The Journal of the Chartered College of Teaching*, and *researchED Magazine*. Meg's work in Mind Brain Education was featured in an episode of the Pew Charitable Trust's *After the Fact* podcast. Meg is an avid traveler and enjoys adventures at home and abroad with family and friends.